ACTA UNIVERSITATIS UPSALIENSIS

Studia Doctrinae Christianae Upsaliensia

30

Cristina Grenholm

Romans Interpreted

A Comparative Analysis of the Commentaries of Barth, Nygren, Cranfield and Wilckens on Paul's Epistle to the Romans

UPPSALA 1990

Distributed by:
Almqvist & Wiksell International
Stockholm — Sweden

Doctoral dissertation at Uppsala University 1990

Abstract

Grenholm, C. 1990. Romans Interpreted. A Comparative Analysis of the Commentaries of Barth, Nygren, Cranfield and Wilckens on Paul's Epistle to the Romans. Acta Univ. Ups. *Studia Doctrinae Christianae Upsaliensia* 30. 154 pp. Uppsala. ISBN 91-554-2529-1.

This thesis deals with the problem of how to explain the different interpretations of Paul's Epistle to the Romans in the four contemporary commentaries of Karl Barth, Anders Nygren, Charles Cranfield and Ulrich Wilckens. The purpose of this study is to put forward and analyse the different interpretations given by the commentators and to examine some ways in which these differences may be explained.

The differences analysed primarily concern central theological issues. A detailed description of the four different interpretations of Romans is given on three levels: (i) concerning Romans 7, (ii) concerning some theological themes in Romans and (iii) concerning some general remarks on Romans which are important for the interpretation of the Epistle.

Different kinds of interpretations are defined by the development of a theory of interpretation which focuses on the arguments supporting the commentators' choices of interpretation. The different interpretations of Romans are explained by reference to the commentators' pursuit of different combinations of kinds of interpretations and by the contents of their arguments. Explanations are also found in their pursuit of different combinations of purposes. Their views of the contents of Christian faith, revelation and the Bible also explain the different interpretations. Special attention is paid to a fundamental lack of clarity in the commentaries concerning the relation between reconstructive and constructive interpretations, the problem of application.

The commentaries are used as examples of biblical interpretation to arrive at a detailed knowledge of the complex process of interpretation. Distinctions are developed concerning kinds of interpretations, kinds of purposes and different views of revelation and the Bible.

Keywords: interpretation, Romans, Barth, Nygren, Cranfield, Wilckens.

Cristina Grenholm, Department of Theology, Uppsala University, Box 1604, S-751 46 Uppsala, Sweden.

ISBN 91-554-2529-1
ISSN 0585-508X

Printed in Sweden
Graphic Systems AB, Göteborg

Contents

Preface

Most dissertations are, I believe, regarded as miracles by their authors. Their miraculous character relates not to their contents, but to their completion. The miracle of the completion of this dissertation overwhelms me with gratitude to some of the people who made worthwhile all the work that went into it.

My special thanks go to Professor Anders Jeffner whose concise critical comments have been a continuous source of inspiration. I also want to thank Professor Lars Hartman for detailed advice, which was especially valuable as the thesis gradually began to take form. Professor Krister Stendahl has taken a continuous interest in my studies, encouraged my endeavours and made me aware at the same time of their limitations by generously sharing with me his international perspective. I also had the privilege of discussing my work with Professor Vincent Brümmer. His views on the kinds of interpretations considerably affected my subsequent reflections.

I want to express my admiration for those who took time to read the manuscript and spent whole days helping me clarify the text and develop my arguments: Docent Carl-Henric Grenholm and Lollo Wijkander.

I would also like to thank all of those who together constituted the important environment in which much more than just the problem of the interpretation of Romans was discussed: the members of the Seminars in Theological and Ideological Studies and New Testament Exegesis, and the scholars and librarians at the University Library.

I also want to give special thanks to Mrs Ray Bradfield, M A. She corrected my English in a manner that added considerably to the worth of this book.

Like all miracles, this one has provided new insights. The degree of patience, understanding and encouragement of my family and friends has surpassed anything I believed possible. I have also been convinced that there is a love which endures all things. For giving me that love I want finally to thank once again my husband Carl-Henric.

Uppsala, January 1990

Cristina Grenholm

Introduction

The history of biblical interpretation is as long as the history of the Bible itself. A decisive turning-point was the rise of the historical-critical interpretation of the Bible, which grew out of the ideas of the Enlightenment. Biblical scholars began to study the Bible with the methods used by other literary interpreters, in particular, historical and philological methods. Hopes were raised for a general consensus as to what the Bible originally meant. According to many, such an exegetical consensus exists today among the majority of biblical scholars. This is stressed not least in various ecumenical documents. The Bible interpreted on historical-critical grounds is held to provide the different confessions with a common base.[1]

Perusal of contemporary biblical commentaries however shows a different picture. Most commentators put forward their interpretations in opposition to interpretations put forward by others. Thus, although a kind of general agreement exists in respect of the methods used, there seems to be less agreement concerning the results. The problem of interpretation dealt with in this study is: why are different interpretations given of the same biblical text? In order to resolve this problem, it is necessary to answer two questions. First, in precisely what way do the interpretations of the commentaries differ from each other? And second, how are we to explain these differences?

The problem of biblical interpretation is dealt with in a broad sense in books of many kinds: methodological introductions, exegetical monographs on the interpretation of a particular pericope, Old and New Testament theologies etc. However, the specific problem dealt with in this study, the problem of the different interpretations of the Bible, is dealt with on the whole in two kinds of literature. The first comprises historical surveys of the main changes in the development of biblical interpretation.[2] The general character of these

---

[1] Cf *Das Evangelium und die Kirche* 1972 p 345. In their search for unity, a Roman Catholic and Lutheran study commission, "Das Evangelium und die Kirche", began their deliberations with a meeting devoted to the question of the gospel and its tradition in the New Testament, "weil man nach der allgemeinen Erfahrung von interkonfessionellen Begnungen, besonders zwischen evangelischen und katholischen Theologen, erwarten konnte, daß bei biblisch-exegetischen Gesprächen die Möglichkeit einer Verständigung besonders groß ist." Cf Betz 1981 p 2. However, e g Räisänen 1987 objects strongly to harmonized interpretations of biblical texts, in his case harmonized interpretations of Paul's concept of law, pp 1–4.

[2] Cf Ingebrand 1966, Grant with Tracy 1984, Reventlow 1986, Gunnlaugur 1988, Morgan with Barton 1988, and Epp and MacRae 1989.

surveys, covering either a long time-span or a large number of interpretations, means that the differences which emerge are not analysed in detail. Consequently, the explanations given relate to characteristic methodological features and lack precision in this respect. The second kind of literature which deals with the problem of the different interpretations of the Bible relates to the theory of interpretation.[3] Attention is focused on the differences in interpretation of the same text, often to the extent of denying the possibility of arriving at a simple interpretation or a limited number of interpretations. Explanations for these differences are found in the interpretation process, which is also carefully analysed. These books nevertheless lack precision in the sense that they penetrate the problem of the different interpretations in the abstract, and do not analyse the interpretations put forward by earlier or contemporary interpreters.

In contrast to these two categories of studies on the problem of the different interpretations of biblical texts, I have chosen another way to come to terms with the question of precisely in what respects the interpretations of biblical texts differ from each other and how these differences are to be explained. I analyse in detail four biblical commentaries on Paul's Epistle to the Romans from the period following the breakthrough of historical-critical exegesis. In this way I can analyse the interpretation process as it actually takes place and seek explanations for the different interpretations not only in a theory of interpretation, but in the different ways in which the interpreters work their way to their interpretations.[4]

The purpose of this study is thus (1) to put forward and analyse the different interpretations of Romans given by four contemporary commentators and (2) to examine whether these differences can be explained, and if so, how. By this, virtually new, approach to the problem of the different interpretations of biblical texts I aim to contribute to the lively debate on the problem of biblical interpretation.

These two purposes raise the questions of what differences to analyse and what kinds of explanations to examine. This study concentrates on the disagreements concerning central theological issues, that is, issues which are

[3] Cf Ricoeur 1980, Frye 1982 and Patte 1983, see also e g Longman 1987.
[4] In many ways the same approach is chosen by Noorda 1989, although his study concerns Lk 4:16–30 and a wider range of commentaries. Young also discusses the problem in a similar way in a recent article, Young 1989. Cf Baird 1981, where five commentaries on Romans (e g the second volume of Cranfield's commentary and the first volume of Wilckens') are reviewed and the question of how historical-critical methods are to be related to the theological application is briefly discussed. An unpublished manuscript by Nordlander also has affinities with this study. See also Pettersson 1988, who analyses examples of interpretations, although in the field of literary criticism, in order to explain different interpretations of the same text. My study also has relevance for the discussion of the different characters of different commentaries. See e g Lohfink 1974 and Schenk 1980. This discussion has, however, by and large merged into the debate on the theory of interpretation, cf Kieffer 1984.

capable of forming part of or initiating theological movements and schools. It is motivated by the fact that it is here that the problem of the different interpretations of the biblical texts becomes important and acute. I therefore focus on problems which relate to systematic theology: the anthropology, the image of God, the view of atonement, eschatology etc.

When it comes to explaining the differences, it seems natural to seek them in the process of interpretation. How do the interpreters of the Bible decide which interpretation to choose? The range of acceptable references (philological, contextual, historical etc) in itself indicates alternative ways of supporting different interpretations. Nor can the possibility be ruled out that the theology of the interpreter and his view of revelation, for example, also influence the interpretation process.

My choice of material for analysis is interlinked with the choice of problem and purposes. Although virtually any commentary could have been analysed for the purpose of describing and explaining the differences in the interpretation of biblical texts, I have chosen to analyse four contemporary commentaries on Paul's Epistle to the Romans. I have also limited my study to commentaries by Protestant authors.

First, the problem of the different interpretations of the Bible has entered a new, and not sufficiently observed, phase following the breakthrough of historical-critical exegesis. Furthermore, the problem has become still more urgent following the disappointments over the biblical interpretation of the liberal theology movement. I have therefore chosen four commentaries from this century.

Secondly, the interpretation of Paul's Epistle to the Romans has been important theologically right through history.[5] Romans is saturated with theological material and therefore well suited for an investigation of the problem of the different interpretations of the Bible with special reference to their relation to systematic theology. For this reason, I have chosen four commentaries on Romans.

Thirdly, the relation between biblical interpretation and systematic theology or expositions of the content of Christian faith is apprehended differently in different traditions. As a result, differences of opinion concerning biblical interpretation are apprehended differently. In Catholic theology the tradition acts as an intermediary link between biblical interpretation and expositions of the content of Christian faith. In Protestant theology the problem of the different interpretations of the Bible becomes more acute, since the sola scriptura principle tends towards a more direct relation between biblical interpretation and exposition of the content of Christian faith.[6] I have therefore

[5] For an extended list of interpreters see Cranfield 1985 (1) pp 30–44.
[6] See e g Fuller 1989. Cf Brown 1985, who deals with the problem of biblical interpretation using church doctrine as his guideline and corrective.

chosen to analyse four commentaries by Protestant scholars.

From all the commentaries still available I have chosen four influential contemporary commentaries. These are Karl Barth's *Der Römerbrief* (first ed 1919, second ed 1922), Anders Nygren's *Commentary on Romans* (Swedish ed 1944, British translation 1952), Charles E B Cranfield's *A Critical and Exegetical Commentary on the Epistle to the Romans* (1975 and 1979) and Ulrich Wilkens' *Der Brief an die Römer* (1978, 1980, 1982).

These commentaries differ from each other in three respects. First, their authors come from different countries and different sectors of the Protestant tradition. Barth (1886–1968) was Swiss, belonged to the Reformed tradition and is probably best characterized as one of the founders of the dialectical theology. Nygren (1890–1978) was a bishop of the Church of Sweden, a Lutheran influenced by the Lutheran neo-orthodoxy. Cranfield (1915–) lives in Scotland and has been a member of the United Reformed Church since 1954, when he left the Methodist Church, in which he had been ordained. Wilkens (1928–) lives in West Germany and has been a bishop of the Lutheran church in Holstein-Lübeck since 1981.

Secondly, their specialities as scholars are different. Barth was Professor of Dogmatics and New Testament theology at Münster 1925–1929 and Professor of Systematic Theology at Bonn 1930–1935. Nygren was Professor of Systematic Theology at Lund 1924–1949. Both were thus systematic theologians. Cranfield and Wilkens, on the other hand, are biblical scholars. Although Cranfield was appointed to a personal chair in Theology at the University of Durham in 1980, all his production lies in the field of biblical exegesis. Finally, Wilkens was Professor of the New Testament at Berlin 1960–1968 and Hamburg 1968–1981.

Thirdly, their commentaries represent different commentary traditions. Barth's makes a fresh start, opposing both the exegesis and systematic theology of his time.[7] Nygren's commentary is in part a reaction against Barth's, but is also critical of modern exegesis, without denying its results.[8] Cranfield's and Wilkens' commentaries are good representatives of the Anglo-Saxon and German traditions respectively. The commentaries also belong to different series, each of which has its characteristics: Nygren's Swedish commentary belongs to the Tolkning av Nya Testamentet series (Interpretation of the New Testament), whose editor Nygren was and which aimed at going beyond contemporary exegetical work and say something about the message of the text. Cranfield's belongs to the International Critical Commentary series (ICC), one of whose distinguishing marks is philological accuracy. Wilkens' commentary forms part of the Evangelisch-Katholischer Kommentar series

---

[7] Cf Lindberg's discussion of the polemical traits of Römerbrief, Lindberg 1969 pp 19–22.

[8] E g Stenström 1984 pp 66f, where a discussion between Stenström and Nygren 1970 is quoted and Nygren characterizes his relation to Barth.

(EKK), one of whose characteristic features is a discussion of the history of interpretation in the two traditions.

Thus, the commentaries chosen are different enough for the problem of the different interpretations of the Bible to be relevant and yet similar enough to prevent the study becoming trivial. However, many spontaneously apprehend a major difference between the commentaries of Barth and Nygren on the one hand and those of Cranfield and Wilckens on the other. Nevertheless, any attempt at a more precise description of this difference is bound to lay bare a complex network of related problems. I therefore treat the four commentaries first and foremost as four interpretations of Romans. This study will show in what respects the commentaries of Barth and Nygren differ from those of Cranfield and Wilckens and consider any similarities which may exist.[9]

My purpose in analysing the differences between the commentaries by Barth, Nygren, Cranfield and Wilckens is set out in part one of this study and my purpose in examining possible ways of explaining the differences is set out in part two. Each raises methodological problems. Some of these are discussed in the introductions to the individual chapters. Something needs to be said, however, about how the different interpretations of the commentaries are set out in part one. In part two I focus on the interpretation process. For this reason, I should also say something about what I mean by interpretation in this thesis and describe at the same time the kind of interpretation I aim at myself.

In order to describe how the commentators' interpretations of Romans differ from each other, I analyse the commentaries on three levels. Chapter one analyses the different interpretations of Romans 7. In chapter two I look at Romans as a whole and the answers of the commentaries to some thematic questions are analysed. Chapter three deals with questions concerning the situation of Paul and of the Romans and questions concerning the purpose, character and theme of the Epistle are taken into account.

Romans 7 was chosen because of the familiar problem of the interpretation of ἐγώ (I). The problem is especially interesting when studying Protestant commentaries, since the traditional Catholic and Protestant interpretations of the passage differ. Ch 7 is also one of the key passages bearing on the much-

---

[9] Barth's commentary has come out in twelve German editions. There are considerable differences between the first and the second editions (1919 and 1922). Since the latter has been the most influential and is the one which has been reprinted, virtually unchanged, I have chosen to analyse it, although in the fifth edition from 1926. Both Barth and Cranfield have shorter versions of their commentaries (Barth 1956 and Cranfield 1987, first ed 1985). However, the original, longer versions suit my purposes better and are also referred to by the authors for a deeper understanding of their interpretations of Romans in the introductions. Other literature by Barth, Nygren, Cranfield and Wilckens has been virtually ignored, since my purpose has been to analyse the commentaries, not the views of the commentators.

debated problem of the interpretation of Paul's concept of the law.[10]

The analysis questions in chapter two were chosen after reading the commentaries by Barth, Nygren, Cranfield and Wilckens and concluding that these were problems with which they dealt in one way or another. A comparison with other commentaries shows that these problems are not unique to these four commentaries.[11] I have also concentrated on problems where the commentaries disagree, since this study concerns the problem of the different interpretations of Romans.

Although the general remarks on Romans analysed in chapter three are not interpretations of the text in the strict sense, but focus rather on the non-literary context of Romans, they are clearly related to the interpretation of Romans. Answering the questions concerning the situation of Paul and the Romans etc forms part of the process of textual interpretation, and the commentators' decisions concerning these issues are closely related to the interpretation of the statements in Romans. The issues raised concern points of conflict between these, and other, commentaries, with relevance for disagreements within systematic theology.

Some of these problems are more explicit than others: for example, the identity of ἐγώ is raised as an explicit problem of interpretation by Barth, Nygren, Cranfield and Wilckens, while the problem of the image of God is less explicit, but nevertheless clearly answered by the commentators.

This threefold analysis avoids several risks. Romans 7 is analysed to avoid the danger of becoming too general. The whole of Romans is taken into account to avoid the risk of being eclectic. Biblical commentaries are seldom read from beginning to end, but are usually used instead as works of reference. The general remarks on Romans are analysed to avoid neglecting questions which are usually asked by exegetical scholars, a risk implicit in the systematic theological perspective that I have chosen.

In order to examine whether the different interpretations of the commentaries can be explained, and, if so, how, I develop a theory of interpretation. Some main features of that theory should be set out here.

A problem of interpretation arises when a statement can be interpreted in at least two different ways. The interpreter has to make a choice. Let me express in a formal way what is meant by interpretation in this thesis: a statement B is an interpretation of a statement A (a) if at least one person P and one situation S are such that B has the same meaning for P in S as A and (b) if the number of possible meanings of B is less than the number of possible meanings of A. The first part of the definition requires that B can make the

---

[10] Cf Räisänen 1987, especially the preface to the second edition pp xi–xxxi.

[11] Barrett 1957, Leenhardt 1957, Kuss 1957 and 1959, Althaus 1966, Michel 1966, Käsemann 1973, Schlier 1977, Achtemeier 1985 and Zeller 1985.

same assertion as A for P in S, i e P cannot at the same time accept B and reject A or vice versa.

The first part of the definition is similar to Arne Naess' definition of interpretation in *Communication and Argument* and includes his criterion of equivalence.[12] The second part of the definition is similar to Naess' definition of precization. According to Naess, all precizations are interpretations, but not all interpretations are precizations.[13] However, I reserve the concept of interpretation for Naess' concept of precization, i e I also regard the second condition (b) as a prerequisite for classification of a statement as an interpretation in this study. I hereby exclude from the concept of interpretation statements which fulfil only the first condition (a) of the definition, e g paraphrases and abstracts. For a statement to be classified as an interpretation it must mean the same as A for P in S *and* it must be less vague and less ambiguous than A.

I thus regard statements as the prime objects of interpretation.[14] Consequently, I regard Romans as being made up of groups of statements which Barth, Nygren, Cranfield and Wilckens interpret. The Swedish philosopher Mats Furberg int al has pointed out that interpretation of a text is not confined to the interpretation of statements, but concerns also the relation between the statements.[15] This I would not deny; but I still hold the statements to be the prime objects of interpretation. However, it is not necessary for my purposes to go any deeper into this discussion of the difference between interpreting statements and interpreting texts.

An interpreter thus makes a choice between different possibilities when he or she interprets a statement. The choice is made by reference to one or more arguments, which differ in form and content. An interpretation may be supported, for example, by reference to the context (a contextual argument) or by reference to the historical situation (a historical argument). By analysing the arguments advanced in favour of an interpretation, it is possible to distinguish different kinds of interpretations and these different kinds of interpretations can serve as possible explanations for the different interpretations of the same text. This is the basis for my attempts to explain Barth's, Nygren's, Cranfield's and Wilckens' diverse interpretations of Paul's Epistle to the Romans in part two.

I call the kind of interpretation aimed at in this study a reasonable inter-

---

[12] Naess 1966 pp 22f and 28.

[13] Naess 1966 pp 39f. Cf Grenholm 1973 pp 26f, where a similar combination of Naess' definitions is used.

[14] Cf Naess 1966 p 14.

[15] Furberg compares the text to the wicker-work of a basket: the interpreter is said to fill in the holes of the wicker-work so that a unity between what is in the text and the different kinds of filling provided by the interpreter constitutes the interpretation of the text. Furberg 1982 pp 116, 165f and 188f.

pretation. For an interpretation to be a reasonable interpretation it should (a) be in accordance with the context of the interpreted statement, (b) take into account the intentions of the author (if known), (c) be in accordance with what most well-informed people hold the interpreted statement to mean, (d) make the text as consistent as possible, i e free from logical contradictions and (e) be as acceptable as possible, i e maximally difficult to refute. In short: a reasonable interpetation R of a statement A is the interpretation which, when compared with other possible interpretations of A, is supported by the most tenable arguments, according to the criteria just mentioned.[16] The reader will be able to evaluate my interpretations of the commentaries from the quotations and references found in the footnotes.

The thesis is disposed as follows: part one sets out the differences between Barth's, Nygren's, Cranfield's and Wilckens' interpretations of Romans. In chapter one I show how differently they interpet Paul's view of Man, the identity of ἐγώ and Paul's view of the law in Romans 7. In chapter two I set out their different interpretations of Paul's answers to questions on some theological themes in Romans. In chapter three I show how the commentaries of Barth, Nygren, Cranfield and Wilckens differ in their understanding of the situation of Paul and the Romans etc, that is, how they differ concerning some general remarks on Romans.

In part two I examine some possible explanations of the differences analysed in part one. In chapter four I develop the theory of interpretation and distinguish between seven kinds of interpretations. Explanations are sought in the different kinds of arguments Barth, Nygren, Cranfield and Wilckens give for their interpretations and in the content of those arguments. The seven kinds of interpretations are further divided into two basic types, reconstructive and constructive interpretations. These are used in chapter five to examine the differences between the purposes of the commentaries and the results they achieve. In chapter six I analyse the contents of the constructive arguments and examine possible explanations for the different interpretations by reference to the answers they give to some basic questions on the content of Christian faith, revelation and the view of the Bible. Finally, I examine the different solutions they give to the problem of application, i e the problem of relating the two basic types of interpretation one to another.

It should be noted that the conclusions given in each chapter are not summaries in a strict sense. In the conclusions I have developed critical remarks and clarified problems found in the analyses.

After reading this book the reader will not be able to solve the problem of the different interpretations of the Bible, but will be made aware of the many dimensions of the problem.

[16] Cf Grenholm 1981 pp 61–64.

PART I:
DESCRIBING THE DIFFERENCES

Chapter One

Interpretations of Romans 7

The commentaries of Barth, Nygren, Cranfield and Wilckens differ from each other both in form and content. My analysis will concentrate on the differences in content. However, attention can be drawn to some other differences, which make the content analysis difficult. The authors refer to the text of Romans in different ways, using the Greek (Cranfield and Wilckens) or translations of the text (Barth and Nygren), in longer (Nygren and Wilckens) or shorter (Barth and Cranfield) units. They also structure ch 7 differently. Barth, Nygren and Cranfield take it as a separate entity. Wilckens includes also 8:1–17, but considers 7:1–6 and 7:7–25 to be two sections of the 7:1–8:17 unity. There is also disagreement over the placing of v 13 in the subsections. Barth and Nygren take it together with the beginning of vv 7–25, while Cranfield and Wilckens group it with the end of the same passage, reading v 13 together with vv 14–25.[1]

In order to be able to compare four commentaries which differ from each other in so many respects, I have analysed a number of other commentaries on Romans so as to identify the central problems of interpretation connected with Romans 7.[2] These concern the three concepts of sin, law and ἐγώ (I), and they are interrelated. I have chosen not to take sin in isolation, but together with the other two concepts. I have also chosen to broaden the question of the identity of the first person singular in this chapter to include anthropology, although in a limited sense. This is motivated by vv 1–6, which clearly do not have an individualistic perspective.

1. Anthropology and the identity of ἐγώ

One problem of interpretation concerns Paul's anthropology as expressed in Romans 7. Following Paul's text, the problem can be divided into two parts. The first is related primarily to vv 1–6 and the second to the verses which follow.

The first problem of interpretation concerns the two kinds of lives depicted

---

[1] Barth 1926 p 222, Nygren 1944 p 284, 1952 p 277, Wilckens 1980 (2) pp 74f and Cranfield 1985 (1) p 340.
[2] Barrett 1957, Leenhardt 1957, Kuss 1957 and 1959, Althaus 1966, Michel 1966, Käsemann 1973, Schlier 1977, Achtemeier 1985 and Zeller 1985.

in 7:1–6 and, according to some, throughout the whole of ch 7. What characterizes them is their relation to Christ. The first kind of life is the life without or before Christ and the second the life with or after Christ. Every attempt to give a name to these kinds of life becomes theologically biased. For example, all lives are now "after Christ" in a chronological sense, but not, according to most theologians, in a qualitative sense. The qualitative aspect of these ideas is related to different views of salvation. In order to be able to analyse the commentaries, and allowing for different interpretations of the qualitative aspects of these two kinds of life, I have chosen to call them "life ante Christum" and "life post Christum". The chronological terms ante and post can then be given different theological interpretations, which relativizes their chronological meaning. The questions are: how do life ante Christum and life post Christum differ from each other and how are they interrelated?

According to Barth's interpretation of Romans 7, life ante Christum is characterized by the actions of human beings now and heretofore, while life post Christum is characterized by God's actions now and heretofore.[3] The difference is as vast as the difference between Man and God; Christ is "die Aufhebung *dieses* Menschen in seiner Totalität."[4] Consequently, human life in this world is life ante Christum. Not even the Christian can step across that border.[5] Theoretically, however, there are different kinds of life ante Christum. A human being as such is "der existentiell gottlose Mensch",[6] but the position of Christians is different. They are aware of their godlessness. Knowing that you are godless is a way of knowing God.[7] This difference is however negligible, according to Barth's interpretation of Paul.[8] All human beings are separated from God and all human beings are aware of this in greater or less degree. Barth writes "Also *das* ist der Mensch: das Wesen, das, wenn es sich, bedrängt von der Problematik seiner Welt, zutiefst auf sich selbst besinnt, die religiöse Möglichkeit hat, die Möglichkeit, das Unmögliche zu wagen, in unerhörtem Übermut zu tun, was es unter allen Umständen nicht tun dürfte, sich zu Gott zu stellen wie zu seinesgleichen."[9] Life ante Christum is a state of disharmony in Barth's interpretation of Paul. Human beings are aware of what they should be, but incapable of attaining it in this world.[10] Since Barth stresses the gulf between God and Man, not much is said in positive terms of

[3] Barth 1926 pp 211–213.
[4] Barth 1926 p 252.
[5] Barth 1926 p 220: "Die Grenze der Religion, ist die Todeslinie, welche scheidet zwischen dem, was bei den Menschen und dem, was bei Gott möglich ist, zwischen Fleisch und Geist, zwischen Zeit und Ewigkeit."
[6] Barth 1926 p 217.
[7] Barth 1926 p 242: "Gott und der Mensch, der ich bin, das geht *nicht* zusammen." See also pp 221f, where Barth makes a distinction between old and new religious possibilities.
[8] Barth 1926 p 217.
[9] Barth 1926 p 226.
[10] Barth 1926 pp 241 and 249.

life post Christum concerning ch 7, except that this human being is the existentially fulfilled Man in the sight of God.[11]

According to Nygren's interpretation of Romans 7, a person is either unrighteous, under the wrath of God, or righteous, liberated from the law through Christ. Life ante Christum is lived under the destructive forces of wrath, sin, law and death, while life post Christum is characterized by freedom from these forces.[12] Life ante Christum and post Christum are named the old and the new aeons by Nygren.[13] Nygren understands Paul to mean that these two aeons are mutually exclusive, since salvation is only possible in the new aeon.[14] Christian life is nevertheless lived in a state of tension between the two aeons here and now.[15]

According to Cranfield, Paul differentiates between life ante Christum and life post Christum by reference to the condemnation of the law. The person who lives ante Christum is under sentence of death because he/she breaks the law.[16] Life post Christum is characterized by liberation from this condemnation.[17] The two kinds of lives are mutually exclusive, primarily because life post Christum is lived with the aid of the Spirit.[18]

According to Wilckens, "Herrschaftswechsel" is the chief means Paul uses to differentiate between life ante Christum and life post Christum. Life ante Christum is characterized by the flesh and life post Christum is characterized by the Spirit. The two kinds of life are mutually exclusive and human beings are removed from the one to the other through baptism.[19] Life post Christum must not be understood as a life free from the law in the sense of freedom from the order that the law is intended to uphold. Rather, it implies freedom from the hopeless state of being condemned to death under the law.[20] How-

[11] Barth 1926 p 211.

[12] Nygren 1944 pp 272–274, 1952 pp 265–267.

[13] Nygren 1944 pp 283f, cf p 21, 1952 p 277, cf p 14.

[14] Nygren 1944 p 309, 1952 p 302: "A Christian is free from the law principally in the sense that he has been justified entirely without the co-operation of the law."

[15] Nygren 1944 p 302, 1952 p 296: "Only if we heed both sides of such facts can we give a true picture of the Christian life; for it is conditioned by the fact that the Christian belongs at the same time to both the new and the old aeons." See also 1944 pp 299 and 301f, 1952 pp 292f and 295.

[16] Cranfield 1985 (1) pp 330f and 352.

[17] Cranfield 1985 (1) p 330: "...a life characterized by freedom from the law, that is, from the law in the limited sense of the-law-as-condemning..." See also p 336.

[18] Cranfield 1985 (1) pp 359f.

[19] Wilckens 1980 (2) pp 62f.

[20] Wilckens 1980 (2) pp 71f (Zusammenfassung). Wilckens denies that he has the same interpretation as Cranfield, p 70 n 281. Wilckens states that Cranfield holds Paul to mean that only the legalistic misuse of the law is abolished and not the law's condemnation in toto. However, Wilckens does not do justice to Cranfield's interpretation. Cranfield stresses that life post Christum is characterized by freedom from the law's condemnation, 1985 (1) pp 330f and 338. At pp 339f, to which Wilckens refers, Cranfield deals with the specific problem of Paul's statement of something negative of the law (7:6), which Cranfield ascribes to legalism. Cranfield and Wilckens however agree on the main distinction between the law and the law's condemnation. Räisänen 1987 pp 42f supports this interpretation of Cranfield.

ever, in Wilckens' interpretation of Romans 7, life post Christum is not perceivable as an earthly reality but belongs to God's spiritual sphere. The act of baptism makes this clear: "Fragt man nach der Wirklichkeit dieses Wunders in der Weltwirklichkeit, 'im Fleisch', so kann die Antwort nur lauten: Sie besteht allein im Geist, der immer der Geist *Gottes* bleibt, wo Menschen, als iustificati impii von ihm ergriffen, in ihm leben und handeln."[21]

The problem relating to 7:7–25 concerns a cluster of problems connected with the identity of ἐγώ in 7:7–25. Who is ἐγώ? In terms of the previous section, is he a person ante or post Christum?[22] The identity of ἐγώ and the different interpretations of σάρξ (flesh) and sin must be related, however, not just to life ante Christum and life post Christum as abstract entities, but also to the intermediate form of Christian life in this world. Christian life and life post Christum refer in what follows to Christian life in this world and its eschatological fulfilment respectively. How are σάρξ and sin interpreted? To what does the tension revealed in v 15 and v 19, for example, refer? An account of the answers of these interpreters to these questions will give us an overview of how they understand the anthropology of Paul in Romans 7:7–25.

According to Barth, this is Paul's description of religious Man in this world.[23] Vv 14–25 voice the experience of what has been said in vv 7–13.[24] This is however the person ante Christum in the sense that he/she is not yet existentially fulfilled. Barth identifies σάρξ with human worldliness, which becomes sinful in relation to God. It is the tragedy of Man that he does not accept and acknowledge this limitation.[25] God wanted to protect Man from the knowledge that he is merely human, but the true immediacy which existed between God and Man has been destroyed and humankind has been thrown into a struggle of opposition in Barth's interpretation of Romans 7.[26] In these circumstances all human endeavour becomes sin, since sin is "die Möglichkeit aller menschlichen Möglichkeiten", while grace is its opposite, God's possibility for humankind.[27] The human possibility of sin is a necessity following the fall of Adam and Eve, according to Barth's interpretation.[28]

---

[21] Wilckens 1980 (2) p 72 (Zusammenfassung).

[22] The problem of how Paul personally is related to ἐγώ is not raised here, since all four commentators reject an exclusive individualistic interpretation. Barth's and Wilckens' interpretations seem to be the more universal, while Nygren and Cranfield keep the person of Paul in view. Barth 1926 pp 224–226, Nygren 1944 e g pp 285 and 298f, 1952 pp 278f and 292, Cranfield 1985 (1) pp 342–347 and Wilckens 1980 (2) pp 76f, 79, and 85.

[23] Barth 1926 pp 226 and 252.

[24] Barth 1926 p 240.

[25] Barth 1926 p 246: "Fleisch heißt beziehungslose Relativität, Nichtigkeit, Nonsens. Das bin ich!" and pp 231f.

[26] Barth 1926 pp 228–231.

[27] Barth 1926 pp 223f.

[28] Barth 1926 pp 233f.

Writing of the dichotomy revealed in 7:15 and 19 Barth says that it is an illusion to suppose that human sinfulness can be limited by a righteous mind. According to his reading of Romans 7, one part of a person cannot be distinguished from another in any meaningful way.[29] Human beings are totally sinful.

Nygren understands Romans 7:7–13 as being about the person living ante Christum and 7:14–25 as being about Christian life in this world.[30] He gives two interpretations for σάρξ. σάρξ is both a characteristic of life ante Christum in contrast to life post Christum, which is characterized by the Spirit, and a characteristic of all human life on earth.[31] Thus a Christian, certainly living a life post Christum in one sense, but not in its fulfilment, shares in the condition common to all men, including the reality of sin, according to Nygren's interpretation. However, the Christian is no longer under the dominion of sin.[32] Thus, σάρξ and sin are almost synonymous in Nygren's interpretation of Romans 7, although a person may be related thereto in three different ways, ante Christum, in Christian life and in life post Christum. Sin is another of the destructive forces under which a person lives ante Christum, but which also affects Christian life on earth.[33] The idea that the Christian is both delivered from and still under attack from sin, for example, explains the tension expressed int al in 7:15 and 19 which should be understood as a picture of Christian life as a life lived in both aeons.[34] That is to say, the Christian lives both ante and post Christum, in Nygren's interpretation of Romans 7.

Cranfield interprets Paul as having given two different descriptions in 7:7–25. First, human life ante Christum is described in vv 7–13. Although Cranfield stresses the Old Testament context, he rejects a strict Jewish interpretation. What Paul is saying in these verses concerns all human beings living ante Christum.[35] Secondly, he depicts mature Christian life in vv 14–25.[36] σάρξ and sin are related to both kinds of lives. In life ante Christum σάρξ refers to "the whole fallen human nature as such . . ."[37] σάρξ characterizes life ante Christum. But Christian life, although not characterized by σάρξ, is not free of it

[29] Barth 1926 pp 244f.

[30] Nygren 1944 pp 295f, 1952 pp 288f.

[31] Nygren 1944 pp 281f, 1952 pp 274f.

[32] Nygren 1944 pp 305f, 1952 pp 299: "Even though through Christ he has been made 'free from sin', so that it is no longer his lord, nevertheless, as long as this life lasts, he still lives under the condition of sin." See further 1944 pp 303–308, 1952 pp 297–301.

[33] Nygren 1944 pp 273 and 299f, 1952 pp 266 and 292f.

[34] Nygren 1944 pp 298–300, 1952 pp 292f and 1944 p 307, 1952 p 301: "Such is the Christian's relation to this aeon. He has the will to do the good, but sin is present with him. In the inward man he desires God's law; but in the realistic situation in which he lives, sin occurs (vss. 21–23)."

[35] Cranfield 1985 (1) pp 342–344.

[36] Cranfield 1985 (1) pp 344–347 and 369.

[37] Cranfield 1985 (1) p 361.

in this world. σάρξ is powerful also in the life of the Christian, although Christians share in the flesh from a totally new point of departure.[38] σάρξ is synonymous with sin in Cranfield's interpretation of Romans 7. In life ante Christum sin is an expression of human self-centredness and self-assertion in opposition to God's law. This is "the inward root of man's outward wrong-doing".[39] Although not totally liberated from sin, Christian life is decisively different from life ante Christum as far as the carnal nature of Man is concerned, since it is not characterized by it. Cranfield stresses that Paul points to the importance of Christian awareness of sin as a consequence of the Christian's insight into the radical demands of the law.[40] Characteristic of Christian life in this world is the tension depicted at the end of ch 7. Only the Christian who knows God's will and is led by the Spirit can experience the tension between God's will and human sin and disobedience.[41]

According to Wilckens' interpretation, ἐγώ is a person living ante Christum as seen by the Christian.[42] The description is universal in being existential.[43] Like Barth, Wilckens believes that vv 14–23 are about the experience of vv 8–11.[44] Wilckens points to the active and moral aspect of σάρξ. As a characteristic of life ante Christum it is sinful, not because the flesh is of less worth than the human spirit, as Platonists held, but because σάρξ makes human beings ante Christum commit sinful acts.[45] Sin makes people disobey God's law.[46] Thus, sin is not human righteousness as opposed to divine righteousness, but human disobedience as opposed to obedience.[47] Since human beings are characterized entirely by their deeds, they are totally sinful and there is no escape from their predicament. According to Wilckens' interpretation, the tension expressed int al in 7:15 and 19 cannot be used by ἐγώ as an excuse.[48] It is deeds that count, human beings are their actions and it is im-

---

[38] Cranfield 1985 (1) p 337: The Christians "are no longer in the flesh in the sense of having the basic direction of their lives determined and controlled by their fallen nature (...), although the σάρξ in the sense of fallen human nature is still an element – and a far from powerless element – in their lives (cf., e.g., 7.14,18,25)." See also p 357.

[39] Cranfield 1985 (1) p 349.

[40] Cranfield 1985 (1) p 366 on 7:24: "The farther men advance in the Christian life, and the more mature their discipleship, the clearer becomes their perception of the heights to which God calls them, and the more painfully sharp their consciousness of the distance between what they ought, and want, to be, and what they are." See also pp 356–358 and 360.

[41] Cranfield 1985 (1) pp 359f and 363.

[42] Wilckens 1980 (2) pp 77 and 96.

[43] Wilckens 1980 (2) p 79.

[44] Wilckens 1980 (2) p 85.

[45] Wilckens 1980 (2) pp 68f and 89. "My members" of v 23 are the action centre of the body, according to Wilckens.

[46] Wilckens 1980 (2) p 91: "Sünde ist Widerspruch gegen das Gesetz;"

[47] Wilckens 1980 (2) p 80: "Nicht weil ich das Gesetz zu erfüllen suche (was ich doch im Sinne des Gesetzes *soll*), bin ich 'unter die Sünde verkauft' (V 14), sondern deswegen, weil ich tue, was das Gebot verbietet."

[48] Wilckens 1980 (2) pp 87f and 91f.

possible for the sinner to fulfil his aims, since he/she lacks the power to do so: sin dominates the sinner.

Many differences thus exist between the commentaries concerning the interpretation of the anthropology of Romans 7. First, the commentators differ in their interpretations of life ante Christum and life post Christum. Barth and Nygren include all aspects of human life, all human endeavour, while Cranfield and Wilckens point to the more limited aspect of the condemnation of the law. However, Barth and Nygren also differ in their interpretations of life ante Christum. Barth points to the gulf that yawns between the human and the divine, while Nygren points to the destructive forces. Cranfield and Wilckens also differ from each other in their interpretations of the condemnation of the law, as indicated by Wilckens' view that life post Christum, i e freedom from the condemnation of the law, is hidden. (See further below on the interpretation of the law.) Furthermore, they all interpret differently Paul's view of the relation of Christian life to life ante Christum and life post Christum. Barth holds that Christian life belongs to life ante Christum, Nygren that it belongs to both life ante Christum and life post Christum and Cranfield and Wilckens that Christian life is essentially life post Christum.

Secondly, the commentators differ in their interpretations of the identity of ἐγώ in 7:7–25. They agree that ἐγώ is a person ante Christum in vv 7–12/13, but they disagree concerning vv 13/14–25. Barth holds ἐγώ to be a person ante Christum, Nygren interprets vv 13–25 as a description of Christian life, Cranfield as a description of mature Christian life and Wilckens agrees with Barth's interpretation. Barth's interpretation furthermore differs from Wilckens' in that Barth includes the Christian, while Wilckens does not; and Nygren's interpretation differs from Cranfield's in that Nygren stresses the ambiguity of Christian life in the two aeons, seeing Christian life as a mixture of life ante Christum and life post Christum, while Cranfield stresses that the characteristic of life ante Christum has been left behind definitively by Christians.

Consequently, they all agree that human beings ante Christum are totally sinful, although Wilckens, in contrast to the others, stresses the active, moral aspect of sin. Because of the different interpretations of ἐγώ, Nygren and Cranfield stress that σάρξ and sin are a part of Christian life, although no longer characterizing life, while Barth and Wilckens reject this interpretation. Nygren's interpretation differs from Cranfield's in that Nygren holds the Christian to be ultimately liberated from the power of sin, his/her conditions of life altered, while Cranfield holds that the Christian is given a new point of departure by a personal change of character. Their different interpretations of the tension implicit in ἐγώ coincide with the other interpretations analysed here. Barth and Wilckens hold it to be of no importance. Barth takes it to be an illusion and Wilckens holds that even if the mind is opposed, it is the deeds that count. Nygren and Cranfield, on the other hand, believe that this tension reflects a profound Christian insight: according to Nygren, the tension is caused by the Christian's awareness that he lives in two aeons and according to Cranfield, it is caused by the Christian's knowledge of the will of God.

2. The law

The second main problem of interpretation is raised by the concept of νόμος (law). Many questions need to be cleared up. Which law does Romans 7 refer to? In what sense is the law holy and good (7:12)? How is sin related to the law (7:7–12/13)? What was the original purpose of the law and what is its purpose in the new situation post Christum?

Barth understands Paul to have a very wide concept of the law. To know the law is to know religion, which is the highest end of which Man is capable. It is thus a general human phenomenon.[49] Religion or the law thus also marks the limit of human potential.[50] The law is good in that it gives human beings experience of God in a negative sense. The law points away from itself to that which alone is good, God. It is also good in that it represents the highest end Man can attain.[51] It points to the strict line which is drawn between the human and the divine.[52] According to Barth's interpretation of Romans 7, the law is related to sin primarily because it reveals that every human possibility is sin, since it is opposed to God. Since the law points to the divine possibility, it makes men aware of their tragic state of existence, of their sin.[53] The law, or religion, also stimulates sin in that it is easily misunderstood. People forget the strict line running between the human and the divine and try to become like God.[54] This is because the instinct of human beings as a species is to try every possibility.[55] Against Schleiermacher Barth holds that religion is not a harmonious state, but a crisis and a dualism.[56] The purpose of the law is thus to point to God's goodness and thereby to show men that the divine possibil-

[49] Barth 1926 p 212: "Ein bald dichterer, bald dünnerer Rauchschleier von Religion liegt über allem menschlichen Geschehen" and p 218: The law, i e religion "ist der *Gipfel* der Humanität – im bedrohlichen Doppelsinn dieses Wortes."
[50] Barth 1926 p 214.
[51] Barth 1926 pp 236 and 238f.
[52] Barth 1926 p 224.
[53] Barth 1926 p 232: The law "wirft auf *alle* andern menschlichen Möglichkeiten das fatale Licht der — Unmöglichkeit." Cf pp 251f on the two laws as an expression of the dualism of human life.
[54] Barth 1926 pp 218 and 231.
[55] Barth 1926 pp 250f.
[56] Barth 1926 p 251: "Religion ist ausbrechender Dualismus." See also pp 235 and 240f.

ity goes beyond all the possibilities of Man.[57] In life post Christum the law has no function, and there is no religion, since life post Christum is the divine possibility, which rescues men from their captivity in a closed human world.[58]

Nygren also interprets Paul as having a wide concept of the law. The law is a destructive force in life ante Christum.[59] The law is good in that it expresses God's will, although it has been largely destroyed in the conditions of life ante Christum.[60] When the good law came up against human sin, it became a destructive force, provoking and increasing sin.[61] The law differs from the other destructive forces – wrath, sin and death – because its purpose was originally good: that of revealing the will of God.

But in life ante Christum its purpose became that of provoking sin, that is, of representing God's opus alienum.[62] So life ante Christum knows the law only as a destructive force. Life post Christum is lived "beyond the realm of the law".[63] According to Nygren, Paul rejects a third use of the law. Christians are liberated from the law in that they are made righteous without it.[64] But Christian life is a life both ante and post Christum as Paul expresses it in 7:21–23 in the passage about the two laws, in Nygren's interpretation.[65]

Cranfield understands Paul to deal both with the Mosaic law and the law represented by the command given to Man in the garden of Eden. This law is holy in its divine origin and authority and just in demanding just conduct and bearing witness to God's justice. That Cranfield's interpretation is closer to the specific Mosaic law is revealed by the way he points out that each commandment of the law is holy.[66] It is through human sin, that is, the misuse and misinterpretation of the good law, that the law has acquired its condemnatory function.[67] The misinterpreted law stimulates and enhances sin.[68] In this way sin becomes a kind of law of its own, "a hideous usurpation of the prerogative of God's law", as Cranfield puts it when commenting on 7:23.[69] The original

---

[57] Barth 1926 pp 239f.
[58] Barth 1926 pp 214f and 252: "Die Wirklichkeit der Religion ist das Entsetzen des Menschen vor sich selbst. – *Jesus Christus* aber ist der neue Mensch jenseits des menschenmöglichen Menschen, jenseits vor allem des frommen Menschen. Er ist die Aufhebung *dieses* Menschen in seiner Totalität."
[59] Nygren 1944 pp 273f and 287, 1952 pp 266f and 280f.
[60] Nygren 1944 pp 287f, 1952 pp 280–282.
[61] Nygren 1944 pp 283f, 1952 p 277 and 1944 p 286, 1952 p 279: "*It is in relation to the law, that sin grows powerful in man.*" See also 1944 p 287, 1952 p 280: "For man being what he is, his encounter with the law always has the effect of giving sin 'opportunity'."
[62] Nygren 1944 p 288, 1952 p 281.
[63] Nygren 1944 p 279, 1952 p 272.
[64] Nygren 1944 pp 282f and 309, 1952 pp 275f and 302.
[65] Nygren 1944 pp 307f, 1952 p 301.
[66] Cranfield 1985 (1) pp 352–356.
[67] Cranfield 1985 (1) pp 338 and 350f.
[68] Cranfield 1985 (1) pp 337f.
[69] Cranfield 1985 (1) p 364.

purpose of the law was to give life, according to Cranfield's interpretation of Romans 7.[70] It is intended to reveal God's will and protect human dignity and liberty.[71] In life ante Christum, however, the law reveals sin's nature and enhances it.[72] The Christian who possesses the Spirit does not necessarily misinterpret the law. He/she is capable of in part fulfilling it.[73] To the Christian the law is also a sign that God will conquer sin.[74] Post Christum Man is liberated from the condemnation of the law, but not from the law in toto. The law is still valid in life post Christum, where the Spirit vouches for its proper use.[75]

Wilckens holds that it is important for the understanding of ch 7 to realize that by νόμος Paul means the Mosaic law, the Torah.[76] The Torah ought not however to be understood in a limited sense, but in a sense that leaves room also for the commandment God gave to Adam, that is, the law that is acknowledged by reason.[77] But νόμος is not to be confused with the political or general order. The law is taken primarily in an eschatological sense. It does not have the function of establishing order, but of ultimately condemning sin.[78] Paul holds the law to be entirely good, according to Wilckens. It does not provoke sin, but only confirms and judges it.[79] By condemning sin and thereby activating its consequences, the law is clearly on God's side. The law not only judges sin as sinful, but also sentences the sinner to death.[80] In opposition to the view that the law makes people sin by encouraging them to strive after their own righteousness, Wilckens holds that Paul states that the law does not make people sin. The law declares that what men have actually done is sin, since they have disobeyed God's law.[81] Thus, the law makes people aware of their sins, but is not to blame. The sinners alone are to blame for

---

[70] Cranfield 1985 (1) p 352 on 7:10: "The true and proper purpose alike of the commandment of Gen 2.16f and of the tenth commandment (representing the whole law) was that man might have life."

[71] Cranfield 1985 (1) pp 350 and 362f.

[72] Cranfield 1985 (1) pp 341 and 354f.

[73] Cranfield 1985 (1) p 356: The law "cannot be properly understood except by the help of the same Spirit by whom it was given. . ." See also p 339.

[74] Cranfield 1985 (1) p 355.

[75] Cranfield 1985 (1) pp 339f and 355f.

[76] Wilckens 1980 (2) p 66.

[77] Wilckens 1980 (2) pp 79, 90 n 376 and p 91.

[78] Wilckens 1980 (2) p 71 (Zusammenfassung): "Nun hat Paulus zwar den Bereich 'im Fleisch' als 'weltweite Dimension' und so auch das Gesetz als 'weltweit wirkende Macht' gedacht. Aber weder hat für ihn das Gesetz eine politische Dimension noch überhaupt seinen Sinn als Welt-*Ordnung*. (. . .) So hat es zwar Herrscher- aber nicht Ordnungs-, sondern Verdammungsfunktion;. . ."

[79] Wilckens 1980 (2) p 84: "Ohne den Verdammungsspruch des Gesetzes hätte die Sünde mir nicht den Tod einbringen können. Aber die Sünde war es, die mir den Tod gewirkt hat, nicht das Gesetz." See also pp 82–84.

[80] Wilckens 1980 (2) p 76.

[81] Wilckens 1980 (2) pp 80f.

their transgressions.[82] Being under sentence of death is a state which Man can do nothing to alter. Therefore the good law cannot fulfil its original purpose. Instead, sinners necessarily continue to sin. This is what Paul means in v 23 by "another law".[83] The law was intended to protect human beings from sin and its fatal consequences.[84] Since men sin, the law condemns them to death irreversibly and the law becomes the master from whom they cannot escape.[85] In life post Christum, however, God is Man's master, because he has annulled the condemnation of the law. Post Christum people can live in accordance with the law. The condemnatory function of the law is abolished, but not the law itself.[86] According to Wilckens' interpretation of Romans 7, the end of the dominion of the law is in accordance with the law itself. The law has dominion over men only until death intervenes; Christians share in Christ's death through baptism and are under the dominion of God.[87] The relevance of this for the actual life of the Christian is limited because God's victory over sin basically belongs to the eschatological fulfilment.[88]

These commentators thus also give different interpretations to what Paul says about the law in Romans 7. First, they give different interpretations of the identity of the law. Barth interprets it anthropologically, understanding it as religion, in the sense of the universal human dilemma of being aware of God, without understanding and respecting the difference between the human and the divine. Nygren interprets the law ontologically as a destructive force controlling people. Cranfield and Wilckens interpret the law in accordance with history of religion as the Torah. However, while Cranfield sees it as the expression of God's will, Wilckens focuses on its eschatological function and rejects any political or world-order meaning.

Secondly, they interpret the way in which the law is good and yet related to sin in different ways. Nygren and Cranfield understand Paul to mean that the law is good in origin, Barth that it is good only relatively, pointing to God who is good, and Wilckens understands Paul to mean that the law is entirely good. According to Nygren and Cranfield, human sin changed the character of the law and turned it into a catalyst for sin. Barth understands Paul to mean that there is a necessary connection between law, i e religion, and sin. It is human nature to try every possibility and yet human beings remain

[82] Wilckens 1980 (2) pp 80 and 91f.
[83] Wilckens 1980 (2) pp 90–92.
[84] Wilckens 1980 (2) pp 82f: "Mit seiner Negation als Verbot des Begehrens sollte es mich vor der 'Bekanntschaft' mit der Sünde (V 7b) und vor ihrer tödlichen Wirkung bewahren."
[85] Wilckens 1980 (2) p 90.
[86] Wilckens 1980 (2) p 70: "Abgetan, veraltet ist also nicht das Gesetz selbst, sondern diese Fluch-Funktion (Gal 3,13) als γράμμα ἀποκτενοῦν, in der es zu unserem Herrn geworden war." See also p 77.
[87] Wilckens 1980 (2) pp 70f (Zusammenfassung).
[88] Wilckens 1980 (2) p 77.

human and therefore sinful. Wilckens takes the opposite view, holding that there is no connection between sin and the law, but since human beings commit sin, and thus transgress against the law, the law condemns them.

Thirdly, concerning the purposes of the law, it is necessary to distinguish between its original purpose, the purpose ante Christum, post Christum and in Christian life. Nygren, Cranfield and Wilckens all understand the original purpose of the law to have been good. Nygren and Wilckens see this purpose as more limited than Cranfield does. Nygren and Wilckens hold that the original purpose of the law was to make known God's will, while Cranfield understands it to be to lead to life. In life ante Christum Barth understands Paul to consider the original purpose of the law: to point to God as well as to reveal human sin. Nygren and Cranfield hold the original purpose of the law to have been changed. In life ante Christum the law has the purpose of provoking sin. Wilckens does not believe that the purpose of the law has changed; it continues to have the purpose of making known God's will. As far as the purpose of the law post Christum is concerned, Barth and Nygren agree that Paul ascribed no function to the law, Nygren, however, in the more limited sense that salvation was obtained without it. Cranfield and Wilckens, on the other hand, interpret the law as having been restored to its proper function in life post Christum. A final difference follows from this. Cranfield and Wilckens understand the law to have been partly restored (Cranfield)/fulfilled (Wilckens) in Christian life, while Nygren regards the Christian as being both ultimately delivered from and still under the dominion of the law which continues to be a destructive force. In accordance with his negative view of Christianity, Barth offers no other interpretation of Christian life and the law than that given concerning life ante Christum and life post Christum.

3. Conclusions

From the analysis of Barth's, Nygren's, Cranfield's and Wilckens' interpretations of Romans 7 we can conclude that they indeed offer different interpretations of the same text. Careful examination showed that every point of comparison revealed at least three and, in most cases, four different interpretations of some central themes of the same chapter of Romans.

We have also seen that as far as many problems of interpretation are concerned, the four different interpretations can be grouped in pairs, although the composition of the pairs varies. On some issues concerning the law, Cranfield and Wilckens interpret the law as having the more limited sense of the Torah or Old Testament law, while Barth and Nygren take it in a wider sense. This means that the interpretations of Cranfield and Wilckens differ from those of Barth and Nygren. This is the case with the problems concerning the interpretation of life ante Christum and life post Christum and the purpose of the law post Christum. However, in the case of the interpretation of the anthropological issues of Romans 7, Barth's and Wilckens' interpretations differ decisively from Nygren's and Cranfield's. This is the case with the problems of the identity of ἐγώ, σάρξ and sin in Christian life and the tension revealed in vv 15 and 19, for example. Furthermore, Nygren's and Cranfield's interpretations differ from Barth's on the one hand and Wilckens' on the other, for example, about whether sin changed the purpose of the law in life ante Christum.

Thus we can conclude that these four commentaries give four different interpretations of the same text of Romans 7 and that sometimes the main point of difference separates the interpretations of Barth and Nygren from those of Cranfield and Wilckens and sometimes separates the interpretations of Barth and Wilckens from those of Nygren and Cranfield.

Chapter Two

Some Theological Themes of Romans

Chapter one analysed and compared the four commentaries of Barth, Nygren, Cranfield and Wilckens on the basis of their interpretations of a certain
chapter in Romans. This manner of comparing commentaries is very natural,
since commentaries follow the biblical text verse by verse. However, another
manner of comparing commentaries on Romans takes as its starting point
Paul's theology and analyses what the interpreters understand Paul to have
said concerning some theological themes which are raised in Romans. This
type of analysis neither presupposes that Paul had a developed theology on
all the major theological issues nor does it presuppose that he systematically
related his theological viewpoints one to another. All it presupposes is that
the text of Romans reflects Paul's own thinking concerning the themes raised
and their theological content. "Paul's theology" here simply refers to Paul's
views concerning aspects of the content of his faith.[1] Bearing in mind this re-
striction of the concept of "theological themes" in this chapter, we can say
that the analysis in this chapter concerns the commentators' interpretations of
the theology of Paul.

As the different theological themes are scattered throughout the text of Romans, comments on the theological themes of Romans are spread out on the
whole in the commentaries and brought out when called for by the text. Exceptions exist in the theological essays of Cranfield and Wilckens, but in their
commentaries, too, much of the interpretation of Paul's theology is spread
out. Thus the material has called for some kind of systematic approach to
make analysis possible. I have chosen to take the three articles of faith, as
generally used in systematizing the contents of books of dogmatics, as my
point of departure. These, having their roots in the reflection on the three
personae of the Trinity, are a classical aid to the systematization of Christian
thinking. Thus, when dealing with the, theologically speaking, comparatively
fragmentary sources of the commentaries, the three articles of faith have
proved most useful when elaborating their various interpretations of the theology of Paul. The advantages of using this classical pattern are several. First,
it helps keep the focus on central theological issues relevant to the problem of
biblical interpretation. Second, it is useful in finding a terminology which is

---

[1] As Räisänen points out, the conviction that Paul's view of the law is ambiguous, or even contradictory, requires a systematic approach. Räisänen 1987 p xxiii.

neither totally dependent on the text of Romans or of the commentaries. Third, it has the advantage of showing how closely interrelated the different theological issues are. Fourth, it gives an idea of how wide is the scope of what can be found in the commentaries. My analysis of this chapter therefore takes its point of departure in the three areas of the three articles of faith.

The first three sections of this chapter correspond to the three articles of faith. They deal with a number of problems of interpretation raised by the text of Romans. The fourth section draws some conclusions from the analysis. A presentation of the problems of interpretation is given at the beginning of each section. It should be noted that since Wilckens differentiates between "Analyse", "Erklärung" and "Zusammenfassung" and also writes excursuses, I have based the analysis in this chapter only on "Analyse" and "Erklärung", when nothing is said to the contrary. Although not explicitly stated in Wilckens' commentary, "Zusammenfassung" and "Exkurs" have a slightly different character, with more comprehensive discussion and occasional reflections concerning the applications of the text. In order to avoid risking that my interpretation of Wilckens concerns what does not belong strictly to the purely exegetical interpretation according to him, I have chosen to raise only the contents of "Analyse" and "Erklärung" in this chapter, although I do not find the lines drawn between the contents of the different sections of Wilckens' commentary to be clear.[2] "Zusammenfassungen" and excursuses are referred to from time to time as clarifications of what has been said in "Analyse" or "Erklärung". For the same reasons Cranfield's concluding essays are not referred to other than in clarification of something in the main text.

1. The old covenant, the character of God and the need for salvation

The whole of the Epistle to the Romans is characterized by Paul's presentation of his gospel against the background of what has now, in a sense, been replaced. This is made very clear in 3:21–26 and the passage about Abraham in ch 4. In part, it deals with the relation between Israel and the new covenant (as in chs 4 and 9–11) and in part with the universal problem of the relation between life ante and life post Christum (as in 1:18–32 and 5:12–21). A number of problems of interpretation are thus raised which belong primarily to the first article of faith concerning, for example, the old covenant and the God of Israel. However, the first article of faith is first only in relation to the other two; the connections are evident with the new covenant, God as saviour

---

[2] Cf *EKK Vorarbeiten* 1969 p 5 in "Vorwort der Herausgeber": "Der der historisch-kritischen Methode verpflichtete Kommentar soll bewußt auf die Gemeinde und die Verkündigung ausgerichtet sein." Cf *EKK Vorarbeiten* 1972 pp 6f.

and salvation. I therefore propose to set out these problems in a way that makes this connection clear. The first problem concerns the identity of the old covenant, its relation to the new covenant and its purpose relative to the purpose of the new covenant. In Romans the old covenant is often represented by the concept of law, νόμος, which is a key to the commentators' interpretations of the old covenant. The second problem is raised by the first and concerns the image of God. It focuses on God's characteristics and the question of whether God has in any way changed attitude towards Man in the new covenant as compared with the old. In books of dogmatics, a doctrine of the fall is generally found within the first article, again as a background for a description of salvation. This corresponds to Paul's concepts of death, the flesh, sin and unrighteousness, for example. The third problem of interpretation concerns the reason why Man needs salvation.

Let us turn first to the problem of the way in which the new covenant is related to the old. According to Barth, Israel's historical covenant with God is only an example of all kinds of religion and primarily of the Christian church.[3] As we saw in chapter one, Barth also includes the era of Adam in the old covenant. The old covenant is both the negative presupposition of the new covenant and its contrast.[4] The new covenant makes a fresh start by negating the conditions of the old covenant. However, the new covenant is also the dialectic synthesis, which overcomes the old covenant and is irreversible.[5] Thus the purpose of the old covenant was to be a precondition of the salvation to be brought forth in the new. The difference between the two covenants is so great however that the new covenant has to be characterized as in some sense a new creation compared with the old.

According to Nygren, Paul holds that everyone who is not of the new covenant is of the old. In Nygren's terminology, those who are not of the old aeon are of the new. Like Barth, Nygren includes also the period from Adam to Moses in the old aeon.[6] But Nygren also gives attention to the problem of God's promises to Israel.[7] The two covenants are opposed to each other since human righteousness in the old covenant is the antithesis of God's right-

---

[3] Barth 1926 pp 314–317. Note also the heading of ch 9 on God's promises to Israel: "Die Not der Kirche".

[4] Barth 1926 p 142: "Und es ist das Nicht-Sein der ersten Welt, das das Sein der zweiten ist, gerade wie die zweite ihren Seinsgrund nur im Nicht-Sein der ersten hat." See also pp 142–144 and 166.

[5] Barth 1926 pp 154f, where it is stressed concerning the Adam-Christ comparison that the covenants are not equivalent, since the dualism is dialectical. This implies that there is only one way: from the first to the second.

[6] The four destructive powers of the old aeon rule "all the world of humanity", Nygren 1944 p 222, 1952 p 215. See also 1944 pp 221–223, 1952 pp 215–217.

[7] Nygren 1944 p 363, 1952 p 361: "Two things are unshakably fixed for Paul: (1) that God gave His promises to Israel, and He never breaks them; and (2) that these promises of God have now been fulfilled in Christ."

eousness in the new.[8] On the other hand the old covenant is God's opus alienum, God's instrument for combatting sin. In this sense the old covenant serves the interest of the new.[9] The old covenant is thus the state of being in which God's purpose of saving mankind has failed, but God still acts. Nygren stresses the lack of continuity between the two covenants (aeons), so that the new covenant has to be understood as something more than a correction of the old, a fresh start.

Cranfield interprets the old covenant in Romans primarily as God's covenant with Israel constituted by the law.[10] The two covenants actually have the same purpose. They both demand faith as well as obedience and faith is said to be the way to the righteousness of the law, i e of the old covenant.[11] However, they do not have quite the same function. The new covenant presupposes the existence of the old: part of the purpose of the old covenant was to make sin manifest, so that God might overcome it in a worthy manner.[12] The old covenant also derives its meaning from the new.[13] The new covenant is thus given priority. God's covenant with Israel was a necessary precondition for the new, but since the two covenants have the same purpose, the new covenant can only be said to be a correction or even a continuation of the old.

Wilckens also interprets the old covenant as God's covenant with Israel.[14] The old covenant failed to attain its purpose of righteousness not because the

---

[8] Nygren 1944 p 21, 1952 p 14: "In the last analysis it is the antithesis between *his own righteousness and the righteousness of God.*" See also 1944 pp 83f, 1952 pp 74–76.

[9] Nygren 1944 p 174, 1952 p 166 on 3:31: "But the righteousness of faith, despite superficial appearances, really works in the same direction as the law, when the law is rightly understood." The law and God's wrath are pictured as God's opus alienum, 1944 p 288, 1952 pp 281f. See also 1944 p 232, 1952 p 225.

[10] Cranfield 1985 (1) p 154, where the law is identified as the Old Testament law and 1986 (2) pp 445f, where Cranfield stresses the Old Testament background and its importance for the understanding of Romans already from the theme in 1:16b–17. However, Cranfield also opens up a wider view on occasion, as we saw in chapter one.

[11] Cranfield 1985 (1) p 171 n 3, where Cranfield identifies νόμον πράσσειν as faith in God and obedience, e g pp 324f, where Cranfield states that in 3:17 Paul stresses the role of obedience in Christian life and 1986 (2) p 508 on 9:31 and the righteousness of the old covenant: "... the way to this righteousness is – faith." It is not surprising that Cranfield opposes Nygren's strict distinction between law and gospel when commenting on the discussion of the interpretation of ἀφωρισμένος in 1:1, 1985 (1) p 54 n 1: "Nygren not only accepts this suggestion without question but goes farther and, interpreting Paul's former separatedness as a matter of separation *for the law*, sees here in the very first verse of the epistle a reference to the 'basic juxtaposition of law and gospel which, from one point of view, is the theme of Romans'. But this is surely *eis*egesis rather than exegesis!"

[12] Cranfield 1985 (1) pp 292f.

[13] Cranfield 1986 (2) p 519: "Christ is the goal, the aim, the intention, the real meaning and substance of the law – apart from Him it cannot be properly understood at all."

[14] This is evident from e g Wilckens' picture of the situation in Rome, Wilckens 1978 (1) pp 41f. There is also no doubt that chs 9–11 concern Israel: 1980 (2) pp 181–185, although there are openings in Wilckens' concept of the law as well as in Cranfield's, cf pp 27–29 above. See also e g Wilckens 1980 (2) p 223.

Jews established their own righteousness, but because through their disobedience they failed to fulfil the demands of the law.[15] Since Man was thus unable to obtain righteousness, God established a new covenant through the creative act in Christ, which fulfilled the purpose of righteousness, not by making Man obedient, but through God's gracious gift of righteousness, i e by faith.[16] Thus the covenants have the same purpose of righteousness, although the old covenant failed of fulfilment. The new covenant is the necessary continuation of the old, which makes good its failure.[17]

Barth's and Nygren's commentaries once again show similarities in their interpretations when compared with those of Cranfield and Wilckens. Barth and Nygren interpret the identity of the old covenant more widely than Cranfield and Wilckens. Barth and Nygren also stress the contrast between the covenants, while Cranfield and Wilckens, although not denying that the new covenant is a result of God's new decisive action, hold that Paul describes a more harmonious relation between them. In Barth's commentary the contrast is related to a dualistic ontology, while in Nygren's the concept of righteousness is decisive. Cranfield's commentary differs from Wilckens' in that he holds that the covenants have different purposes, while Wilckens intimates that the new covenant was established by God because the old failed to achieve its purpose of making Man righteous. Furthermore, Barth's and Nygren's interpretations of Paul stress that the new covenant was a fresh start, setting new conditions for the whole of creation, while Cranfield and Wilckens understand Paul differently. They hold rather that the conditions of the world are very much the same, although the new covenant has made possible a correction, so that Man may live in accordance with the original purposes of creation.

Secondly, let us analyse Barth's, Nygren's, Cranfield's and Wilckens' interpretations of the image of God which Romans gives. According to Barth's interpretation, God is totally different and therefore unknown and unfathomable.[18] God is also truth.[19] Therefore God can only appear to the world as its judge if he is to remain God.[20] However, God's prime characteristic is his faithfulness.[21] This is shown in the new covenant, where by judging the world

[15] Wilckens 1978 (1) pp 176f.
[16] Wilckens 1978 (1) pp 327f.
[17] Wilckens 1978 (1) pp 156f and 1980 (2) p 223: "Das Ziel ist zwar Christus, nicht die Tora; aber die Gerechtigkeit, die Christus dem Glaubenden schafft, ist ja ursprünglich eben das Ziel der Tora, das diese jedoch Sündern gegenüber zu verwirklichen 'zu schwach war' (8, 3)."
[18] Barth 1926 p 18: "Gott! Wir wissen nicht, was wir damit sagen." See also pp 315f and 408.
[19] Barth 1926 p 54: "*Gott* is wahr; (...) *nicht* der Mensch ..." and p 225 where Barth differentiates between human reality, "Wirklichkeit", and divine truth, "Wahrheit".
[20] Barth 1926 p 65: "Und gerade der Blick auf Gott den Richter zeigt die einzige positive Beziehung zwischen hier und dort, ..."
[21] Barth often translates πίστις "Treue Gottes", Barth 1926 p xvii. See also p 54, where it is stated that "Gottes Treue kann getäuscht, aber nicht aufgehoben werden."

in his righteousness, God remains faithful and forgiving to Man, letting his righteous wrath be shown to be less persistent than his love; God is "Ja und nicht Nein".[22]

Nygren also holds that the decisive characteristic of God, according to Romans, is his love, agape (ἀγάπη). God's love is wholly grounded in himself and different from human love.[23] God is sovereign, since his love is free. God is free both to love whomever he chooses and to reject whomever he chooses.[24] All this makes God totally different from Man. Since God's love does not rely on any advantages of the loved one, God can also love the sinner and by this means divine love overcomes divine wrath in the new covenant.[25]

Cranfield gives a more dualistic picture of Paul's opinion. God's two characteristics are his righteousness and his love, in the sense that God is both hostile toward sinful Man and merciful, in that he has a plan to redeem them. God's hostility is brought to an end in the new covenant.[26]

Wilckens draws the same tense picture of a God who is both benevolent and severe in his grace.[27] His compassion however triumphs over his wrath.[28] In Wilckens' interpretation of Romans this is an expression of God's faithfulness to the covenant which is stressed also in the new covenant.[29]

Thus, these four commentators understand Paul's picture of God in Romans in two different ways. Cranfield and Wilckens give a dualistic picture of a God, who is both loving and severe. Barth and Nygren, although not denying the wrath of God, give a more monistic picture of God, pointing to the prime characteristic of love. Barth and Nygren also stress the view that Paul holds God to be totaliter aliter, totally different from anything in this world.

---

[22] Barth 1926 p 67. See also pp 68 and 156.

[23] Nygren 1944 pp 201–207, 1952 pp 196–202, where this view of God's love is contrasted with that of Augustine. Cf Barth 1926 pp 303f, where God's agape is opposed to eros.

[24] Nygren 1944 pp 368f, 1952 pp 366f.

[25] Nygren 1944 pp 206f, 1952 pp 200f, and 1944 p 196, 1952 p 191: "Where the righteousness of God rules there is no longer room for the wrath of God."

[26] Cranfield 1985 (1) pp 267f: "It was διὰ τοῦ θανάτου τοῦ υἱοῦ αὐτοῦ that we were reconciled to God, because, on the one hand, Christ's death was the means by which God pardoned us without in any way condoning our sin and so laid aside His hostility towards us in a way that was worthy of His goodness and love and consistent with His constant purpose of mercy for us, and, on the other hand, it was the means by which He demonstrated His love for us and so broke our hostility toward Himself." Cf 1986 (2) pp 828f (essays).

[27] Wilckens 1980 (2) pp 247f: "Güte und Strenge sind, (...) zwei Aspekte seiner Gnade ..."

[28] Wilckens 1978 (1) pp 297f, where Wilckens characterizes Paul's view of atonement in opposition to the apocalyptic view of salvation thus: " ... weil *Gott* (der Richter) den eschatologischen Zorn 'über alle Gottlosigkeit und Ungerechtigkeit der Menschen' (1,18) im Sühnetod Christi statt an den Sündern an Christus vollstreckt hat, weil darin Gottes heilschaffende *Gerechtigkeit* als seine *Liebe* zu seinen Feinden zur Wirkung gekommen ist."

[29] Wilckens 1978 (1) p 196 on 3:21–26: "So wird dieser zum Erweis seiner Gerechtigkeit, als seiner heilschaffenden Bundesgerechtigkeit, die alle Menschen als Sünder ihr zueignet, indem sie ihre Sünde durch die Sühne in Christi Tod *aufhebt*."

Thirdly, we turn to the question of what caused the need for salvation. According to Barth, Paul perceives the need for salvation in that Man is human and created, although this does not imply that Man was created sinful.[30] Sin is the force that makes individuals – or the church – neglect the distinction between the human and the divine. They think that they can recover their lost unity with God unaided and seek to establish their own righteousness.[31] Sinful men also rob God of his divinity, treating God as an object of this world.[32] One might say that the need for salvation is caused by men's ignorance of the distinction between the human and the divine, which makes them both seek to establish their own righteousness and diminish God to the human and worldly.

According to Nygren, Paul states that although God has revealed himself, he has not been recognized.[33] God has therefore abandoned men to the four destructive forces of wrath, sin, law, and death. Unrighteousness is thus not just a moral quality. Rather, it is the turning aside of Man from God. The consequence of human unrighteousness is the state of submission to the forces of destruction.[34] It was this state that brought about the need for salvation.

Sin is a force that controls Man "as a result of the corrupt nature inherited from Adam", according to Cranfield's interpretation of Romans.[35] Sin makes men disobey the law.[36] Sin thus becomes disobedience to God's law and this gives rise to the need for salvation.[37]

Wilckens says sin is an almost personified force. It has dominion over men and is universal.[38] This does not make men innocent, however. People are responsible for their sins.[39] Sin is basically transgression of the law, the violation of the agreement between God and his people in the old covenant. Men need to be saved from the consequences of their transgression of the law.[40]

Thus, these four interpreters all agree that in Romans sin is seen as a force.

[30] Barth 1926 p 63: "Fleisch" is given the interpretation "Unreinheit" and "Nur-Menschlichkeit". See also pp 292 and 229–231 on the original state of life in Paradise.
[31] Barth 1926 pp 145f and 151f, where the law is said to be a reminder of Man's lost unity with God, which makes men seek their own righteousness. See also pp 356–358 about the sin of the church.
[32] Barth 1926 p 19: "Wir meinen zu wissen, was wir sagen, wenn wir 'Gott' sagen. Wir weisen ihm die höchste Stelle in unser Welt zu. Wir stellen ihn damit grundsätzlich auf eine Linie mit uns und mit den Dingen."
[33] Nygren 1944 p 112, 1952 pp 106f.
[34] Nygren 1944 pp 115–118, 1952 pp 109–112.
[35] Cranfield 1985 (1) p 275, see the whole section pp 274–279 and 191.
[36] Cranfield 1985 (1) pp 292f.
[37] Cf Cranfield 1986 (2) p 850 (essays): The law "sets the necessary forensic stage on which Christ's saving work is wrought . . ."
[38] Wilckens 1978 (1) pp 172f.
[39] Wilckens 1978 (1) pp 316f. Wilckens holds that Paul does not distinguish between sin as fate and sin as something for which human beings are responsible.
[40] Wilckens 1980 (2) p 91: "Sünde ist Widerspruch gegen das Gesetz" and 1978 (1) pp 132f.

However, they differ about the effect that sin has on human beings. The prime difference between the interpreters might be said to concern the moral aspect of these consequences. Cranfield's and Wilckens' interpretations point toward emphasis of the moral aspect, i e the transgression of the law, while Barth and Nygren widen their interpretations to include more than just moral shortcomings.

2. Atonement and righteousness

Of course the principal character in Romans is Jesus Christ and its essential matter, the gospel of God's act of salvation in and through him. Subsequent theological reflection has carefully penetrated every conceivable idea concerning Jesus Christ in relation to the second article of faith: the nature of Jesus Christ in christologies, the meaning of his life, death and resurrection in the different doctrines of atonement, the effects of his saving work in different interpretations of righteousness etc. This article of faith contains many problems of interpretation. I have singled out four:

The very theme of Romans 3:21–26 brings us up against one of the classical cruxes of atonement: how did Christ bring salvation to Man? This problem is closely related to the problem of why God became human or what caused him to intervene in this manner. These two problems focus primarily on the actions of God. Then we have the recipients' side of the matter. One of the most frequently used words in Romans is δικαιοσύνη (righteousness). God's righteousness has been granted to all who believe (3:20, 5:8–9 etc). I put the problem thus: what is righteousness? Aware that this concept refers to a relation, I would like here to bring out the commentaries' interpretations of this relation including God and Man, the two partners in the relationship. The last problem brings us to the heart of Protestantism: how does Man obtain righteousness? Although the answer of the Reformers was derived at least in part from Romans, Protestant commentators have been compelled to take their stand on the text itself and the continued urgency of the question. What is Paul's opinion really? The problem concerns the relationship between faith and works and the problem of imputation, i e whether people are made righteous or just declared to be so. Also contained in the problem is of course the question of the interpretation of faith and works.

Let us start with the problem of how Jesus brought salvation to human beings. According to Barth, Paul states that salvation is a matter of abolishing all that is human and worldly. This becomes a reality in the death of Christ.[41]

---

[41] Barth 1926 p 144: "... alles das, was in dieser Welt auf eine Überwindung und Erneuerung dieser Welt hinweist, nur als Tod erscheinen ..." and this is why Christ in the flesh has to die in order to be established as the son of God. See also pp 128f, where faith is said to be a power which extinguishes the believer, here Paul.

But this is only the antithesis. The irreversible synthesis is realized in the resurrection of Christ. The salvation of God triumphs over the judgment of God.[42] In the resurrection of Christ the true relationship between Man and God is revealed and established as the life of the new Man, "die Existentialität des neuen, in Gott lebenden Menschen."[43] Human beings are fulfilled existentially in Christ.

According to Nygren's interpretation of Romans, Jesus Christ has overcome the four destructive forces: wrath, sin, law and death, which have the dominion over this aeon. The victory of Christ is interpreted also as a cosmic triumph, giving the idea of a cosmic drama. In this drama God's terrible wrath is overcome by his love.[44] The revelatory aspect of the Christ event is also brought out, as it is in Barth's commentary.[45]

Cranfield gives a different answer. Jesus Christ became the object of God's wrath toward sinful men, thus liberating them from his own enmity at his own expense, according to Romans.[46] However, Christ also bore human enmity to God in his passion. This was the deepest humiliation, since human enmity to God is "totally irrational and inane".[47]

Wilckens answers the question in two ways. First, the death of Christ is understood as a sacrifice. There is a difference between Paul and Anselm however. Paul sees this sacrifice not in a forensic but in a cultic context.[48] Through this sacrifice God abolishes sin, or, more precisely, the consequences of human sin.[49] Through the death and resurrection of Christ, God's righteousness, including his love, triumphs over the power of sin and makes possible the justification of the sinner.[50] Secondly, the atonement is viewed as the negation of the negation of judgment, the dialectical synthesis which

[42] Barth 1926 p 168: "Die Einheit des göttlichen Willens spaltet sich zur Zweiheit, um sich in der Überwindung dieser Zweiheit um so siegreicher als Einheit zu erweisen." See also pp 169 and 178f.

[43] Barth 1926 p 265, see also pp 259–266.

[44] Nygren 1944 pp 28, 163 and 197f, 1952 pp 20f, 155f and 192f.

[45] Nygren 1944 p 166, 1952 p 158: "We must notice how central is the idea of manifestation, the public presentation and demonstration, in this passage 3:21–31."

[46] Cranfield 1985 (1) p 217 on 3:25–26: "We take it that what Paul's statement that God purposed Christ as a propitiatory victim means is that God, because in His mercy He willed to forgive sinful men and, being truly merciful, willed to forgive them righteously, that is, without in any way condoning their sin, purposed to direct against His own very Self in the person of His Son the full weight of that righteous wrath which they deserved."

[47] Cranfield 1986 (2) p 734, see also p 733.

[48] Wilckens 1978 (1) pp 195f. Cf pp 201f (Zusammenfassung) and the excursus "Zum Verständnis der Sühne-Vorstellung" pp 233–243.

[49] Wilckens 1978 (1) p 186: "Sofern Gottes heilschaffende Gerechtigkeit sich Sündern zuwendet, kann dies nur so geschehen, daß deren Verurteilung, die das Gesetz ausspricht, durch die Offenbarung der Gottesgerechtigkeit aufgehoben wird."

[50] Wilckens 1978 (1) pp 184–187, cf p 73 (Zusammenfassung).

abolishes the contrast between God's wrath and his righteousness.[51]

Thus, once again, there is a difference between Barth's and Nygren's interpretations of Romans and those of Cranfield and Wilckens. Cranfield and Wilckens focus on the circumstance that Christ vicariously took upon himself the sinners' punishment, although this idea is modified in Wilckens' interpretation by the cultic setting. Barth and Nygren, on the other hand, stress the revelatory aspect. Instead of interpreting Paul's view of how Jesus Christ brought salvation to Man in terms of God's wrath and Man's satisfaction, Barth and Nygren hold that through Christ God altered the conditions of human existence in a way that changed the whole ontology. This happened through and was revealed in Christ. It should be noted that both Barth and Wilckens make use of dialectical terminology.

Secondly, let us analyse why God became a human being. In Barth's interpretation, God had two reasons for doing what he did in Christ. First, God is God and his prime characteristic is faithful love effective as mercy to sinful Man.[52] Secondly, in Christ God revealed what humans failed to acknowledge, because they lacked true knowledge: God judges all that is human, but he is also merciful and salvation is available.[53]

As stated above, Nygren shares Barth's interpretation of the revelatory importance of God becoming a human being. Nygren also explains God's action in Christ as a consequence of God's love and rejects the view that Paul asserts that this was essential so as not to violate God's righteousness.[54]

According to Cranfield, Paul holds that God had to act like this so as not to violate either his own righteousness, or human responsibility.[55] God in his righteousness punishes human sin in Christ. By not punishing humanity, God shows his love and mercy.[56]

According to Wilckens, Paul explains why God chose to become a human being by reference to the sacrifice. But God did not punish Man because he was guilty of sin, as Anselm and others believed, but took the reality of sin on himself vicariously in order to be rid of its consequences.[57] God's sacrifice of

---

[51] Wilckens 1978 (1) p 324 on grace: "Sie *negiert die Negation* des κατάκριμα !". Cf p 330 (Zusammenfassung): "*Die Aufhebung dieses Gegensatzes als Negation der Negation ist das Wesen der Versöhnung.*"

[52] Barth 1926 pp 70–72 and 378.

[53] Barth 1926 p 81: "Gottes Gerechtigkeit hat sich uns in ihm (Jesus) erwiesen, gezeigt. Wir sind durch ihn in den Stand gesetzt, die Geschichte (...) von Gott aus zu sehen, im Lichte seiner alles aufhebenden Barmherzigkeit." See also p 177: "Sofern wir uns selbst als Verwandte des Christus (in seinem *Todes*weg) erkennen, schauen wir das Unanschauliche: das Erbarmen Gottes, uns selbst als seine Kinder, ..."

[54] Nygren 1944 pp 166f, 1952 pp 158f: the death of Christ is a revelation of God's righteousness, and 1944 pp 205–207, 1952 pp 200–202: the death of Christ is a proof of God's love.

[55] Cranfield 1985 (1) p 200: Human responsibility is very important, since Man is "His morally accountable creature". See also pp 266–268.

[56] Cranfield 1985 (1) p 264, cf 1986 (2) pp 829f (essays).

[57] Wilckens 1978 (1) pp 195f.

41

his own son is not taken to be the required prize, as in Anselm, but an act of God's powerful love, revealing the nature of his loyalty to the covenant, which is his righteouness.[58]

Thus Barth and Nygren give similar interpretations of Romans on this issue: God became a human being because he wanted to reveal his love. Because this was totally different from human love revelation was necessary. Cranfield and Wilckens give different explanations, although they point in the same direction. Cranfield understands Paul to view God's prime motive in moral terms. God managed hereby to resolve the moral predicament of having either to prove himself unrighteous or not hold mankind responsible. The same predicament underlies the solution which Wilckens believes Paul to be putting forward, but taking into account the cultic context, it would be wrong to use forensic terms. Other means exist in the cult to make wrongs right.

Thirdly, we turn to the problem of interpreting what righteousness is in Romans. Only God is righteous, according to Barth's interpretation. God's righteousness expresses itself in that he remains what he is – merciful, not condemnatory – whereby men obtain forgiveness.[59] Men are declared righteous without being made righteous, i e without being changed in any conceivable way. Righteousness is part of the reality of God, which is not at the disposal of human beings. According to Barth, however, God's reality is "more real" than the world's and thus humans are what they are not.[60]

According to Nygren's interpretation, righteousness is the new objective state of being, granted to Man through Christ. It is characterized by liberation from the destructive forces of this world and is not to be interpreted in moral terms.[61] Nygren thus neither interprets Paul's concept of righteousness as a divine characteristic nor as a human quality, but as something which characterizes the new reality which has come through Christ.

As was seen above, Cranfield holds that, according to Romans, God's righteousness is mainly God's justice: since human beings are characterized by their moral responsibility, it is God who holds them responsible and punishes

---

[58] Wilckens 1978 (1) p 196: "So wird dieser zum Erweis seiner Gerechtigkeit, als seiner heilschaffenden Bundesgerechtigkeit, die alle Menschen als Sünder ihr zueignet, indem sie ihre Sünde durch die Sühne in Christi Tod *aufhebt.*" See also pp 292f.

[59] Barth 1926 pp 67f.

[60] Barth 1926 p 76: "Er erklärt *seine* Gerechtigkeit als die Wahrheit hinter und über aller Gerechtigkeit und Ungerechtigkeit der Menschen" and p 77: "Wirklich ist und bleibt 'unsre' Gerechtigkeit nur als *Gottes* Gerechtigkeit." See also p 96, where Abraham is said to *be* what he is *not* as a believer. The same idea is expressed concerning 12:9b, p 439, where to cling to that which is good is to love one's neighbour through ". . . das Erwählen dessen, was *er nicht ist* . . ."

[61] Nygren 1944 p 84, 1952 p 76: "This righteousness is not merely something individual; it is the universal mark of the new age, of God's kingdom which has come through Christ." See also 1944 pp 82–85 and 314f, 1952 pp 74–77 and 307f.

their transgressions. Human righteousness is a new state of being. Cranfield states that, according to Paul, this is not a moral transformation.[62] But he also says that, according to Paul, human free will is restored, i e "the freedom to obey God".[63] It is not quite clear what this status is apart from its moral implications, but one important answer is to be found in the heading of 7:1–6 "Freedom from the law's condemnation". Human righteousness is the state of not being condemned.[64] Cranfield is thus not consistent when he interprets Romans on this issue. When compared, for example, with Barth it is clear that Cranfield's commentary stresses the moral aspect. Although he does not hold the state of freedom from condemnation to be identical with the moral transformation of the believer, he stresses the connection between justification and a new ability to fulfil the law.[65]

According to Wilckens' interpretation, God's righteousness in the old covenant is God's faithfulness to his covenant, i e to those who obey him, the righteous. However, when developed by Paul in respect of the new covenant, God's righteousness is his eschatological power of salvation, which includes the justification of sinners.[66] Human righteousness is primarily a gift from God, which liberates Man from the dominion of sin.[67] Righteousness is thus interpreted as God's power, to which men can relate and which characterizes the sphere of the covenant.

Righteousness is a relational term, but it is possible to stress different aspects of the relationship. First, it is possible to stress the divine side, holding that righteousness is primarily a characteristic of God. Secondly, it is possible to stress the human side and hold that righteousness is a human quality obtained in the righteous relationship with God. Thirdly, it is possible to point primarily to the relationship itself, which was unrighteous, but has become righteous through Christ. In this case the state of things is changed. The first sense of the term righteousness I call theocentric, the second anthropocentric and the third the ontological meaning of righteousness. Of these interpreters, Barth interprets righteousness in Romans in a theocentric sense, Cranfield in an anthropocentric and Nygren and Wilckens in an ontological sense.

Finally, let us analyse how Barth, Nygren, Cranfield and Wilckens solve

[62] Cranfield 1985 (1) p 95: ". . . there seems to us to be no doubt that δικαιουν, as used by Paul, means simply 'acquit', 'confer a righteous status on', and does not in itself contain any reference to moral transformation."

[63] Cranfield 1985 (1) p 90. For the close relation between righteousness as a state of being and its moral implications see p 256, where they are said neither to be identical, nor to be the one a consequence of the other, but "justification necessarily involves reconciliation."

[64] Cranfield 1985 (1) p 28.

[65] Cranfield 1985 (1) pp 371, 378 and 393.

[66] Wilckens 1978 (1) pp 165f. Wilckens gives a lengthy discussion of this in the excursus "Gerechtigkeit Gottes", pp 202–233, see e g p 204.

[67] Wilckens 1980 (2) pp 16f, cf 1978 (1) pp 205–208 (Zusammenfassung).

the problem of interpreting how righteousness is achieved by human beings in Romans. According to Barth, Paul understands Man to be righteous in and through faith. It is characteristic of faith that it is based not on the reality of this world, but on God's reality: faith is a leap into the unknown.[68] In faith human beings are even abolished as themselves, as they know themselves, and established as what they are not, i e as the new human being, as Christ.[69] Faith is no work of Man, it is God's acknowledgement of Man. Men are declared righteous forensically.[70] Righteousness is thus achieved through faith, with all human endeavour excluded.

According to Nygren, Paul understands the heart of the matter to be that human beings are justified exclusively by faith, which excludes every human contribution.[71] To believe is to be "gripped and constrained by God's power, and thereby borne into the new age, into life with Christ".[72] It is a characteristic of faith that it has nothing human to rely on, but relies entirely on God's promises.[73] Nygren holds that, according to Paul, human beings are declared righteous in that they are brought into the new covenant, but that righteousness is nevertheless not a human quality. Christians are rather brought into the ontological state of righteousness.

Cranfield, too, holds that righteousness is obtained solely by faith, according to Romans.[74] Even faith is an openness to God, which God creates in human beings.[75] It is a characteristic of faith that it is not dependent on human potential, but relies entirely on the promises made by God.[76] Human beings are declared righteous and are also morally transformed. Cranfield holds that Paul avoids two misunderstandings by maintaining a difference and a proximity between justification and moral transformation. First, good works are not to be apprehended as a means of obtaining righteousness and thus becoming justified through personal merit.[77] Second, good works are not to be apprehended either as totally separated from justification.[78] Paul avoids the misunderstanding of legalism by holding that the law must be fulfilled in faith, this

[68] Barth 1926 pp 33, 72f and 128f.
[69] Barth 1926 p 121: faith is participation in "der Negation der Negation" and p 125: "Wir sind nicht nur, was wir sind, wir sind durch den Glauben, was *wir nicht* sind." See also pp 478f.
[70] Barth 1926 p 76: "Forensischer, ursach- und bedingungsloser, nur in Gott selbst begründeter Spruch ist diese Erklärung, *creatio ex nihilo*, Schöpfung aus dem Nichts." See also pp 140, 187 and 196.
[71] Nygren 1944 p 87, 1952 p 79: " 'Through faith', ἐκ πίστεως, is Paul's usual phrase when he speaks about justification. He means to preclude all thought of a righteousness of our own, attained through law and works, ..." See also 1944 pp 156–163, 1952 pp 149–156.
[72] Nygren 1944 p 86, see also pp 79f, 1952 p 78, see also pp 71f.
[73] Nygren 1944 pp 187f, 1952 pp 178–180, when commenting on the Abraham story.
[74] Cranfield 1985 (1) pp 100 , 103 and 220.
[75] Cranfield 1985 (1) p 90.
[76] Cranfield 1985 (1) p 248.
[77] Cranfield 1985 (1) pp 221f.
[78] Cranfield 1985 (1) p 95.

being "the meaning of the believer's liberation".[79] According to Cranfield, Paul thus seems to hold both that Christians are declared righteous and that they are actually made righteous. Let me put it this way: human beings are declared righteous within a moral context.

Wilckens also asserts that Paul understands humans to be justified by faith. Faith is reliance on God's promises, not a personal attitude.[80] In accordance with the dialectical scheme, however, although human beings are justified by faith alone, good works are not excluded.[81] This is explained by Wilckens' interpretation of good works and condemnation. According to him, human beings are not condemned because they establish their own righteousness, but because they fail to do so.[82] Wilckens rejects the forensic understanding of justification and asserts that the cultic context makes it clear that something actually happens through the sacrifice of Christ. The believers are made righteous.[83] Righteousness appoints new premises for the present state of existence. They are brought into the ontological state of righteousness, which includes a moral transformation.

Thus, Barth and Nygren agree in their interpretation of Romans. Human beings are made righteous by faith alone and they are declared righteous. Cranfield's interpretation differs from those of Barth and Nygren in that he believes Paul means that human beings are not only declared, but also made, righteous and are morally transformed. Wilckens' interpretation differs still more from Barth's and Nygren's. Wilckens sees no contradiction between faith and works or between human righteousness and the righteousness of God. When men failed to establish their own righteousness, God gave it to them. Justification therefore also includes moral transformation.

---

[79] Cranfield 1985 (1) p 383. See also p 384.

[80] Wilckens 1978 (1) pp 89 and 193f. Cf the excursus p 208.

[81] Wilckens 1980 (2) p 129, clarified in the excursus: "Das Gericht nach den Werken II (Theologische Interpretation)" 1978 (1) pp 142–146, e g p 144: "Denn es sei eine falsche Paulusexegese, die den Glauben als Gegensatz zum Wirken versteht." See also p 330 (Zusammenfassung) for 5:12–21: "Erst hier klärt sich das Verhältnis, in dem die beiden einander *entgegenstehenden* Aussagenreihen über die Offenbarung des Zornes und der Gerechtigkeit Gottes, über Sünde und Rechtfertigung, Werke und Glaube, Gesetz und Gnade *aufeinander bezogen* sind. Der Begriff, der die Einheit dieses widersprüchlichen Verhältnisses bezeichnet, ist der der *Versöhnung*."

[82] Wilckens 1978 (1) pp 132f, clarified in the excursus "Das Gericht nach den Werken II (Theologische Interpretation)", pp 142–146, especially p 145: "Nicht das Tun von Werken, sondern die böse faktische Wirklichkeit, die die Werke des Sünders angerichtet haben, ist in der Glaubensgerechtigkeit aufgehoben."

[83] Wilckens 1980 (2) pp 22 and 129f, developed in the excursus "Das Gericht nach den Werken I (Traditionsgeschichtliche Voraussetzungen)" 1978 (1) pp 127–131 and the excursus "Zum Verständnis der Sühne-Vorstellung" pp 233–244, especially p 243.

3. Christian life and eschatology

The third article deals for example with Christian life in this world and eschatology. Romans deals with these issues int al in 6:15–23, 8:1–39 and 11:25–15:13.[84] Leaving aside the problem of how we are to interpret Paul's view of baptism and other matters, I raise only two problems of interpretation in this section. The first concerns the characteristics of Christian life in this world, a question intimately connected with the interpretation of the eschatological fulfilment of Christian life. The character of Christian life as something already present and yet not fulfilled offers different possibilities for interpretation. The second problem of interpretation therefore concerns these commentators' view of Paul's understanding of the eschatological fulfilment and its relation to present reality, as expressed in Romans.

First, let us examine how the commentators interpret the characteristics of Christian life in Romans. The righteousness of Christians cannot be perceived in this world, according to Barth's interpretation.[85] Through the revelation in Christ it is possible nevertheless to know something about the existentially fulfilled life of Christians with God. Existentially, Christians are at God's disposal and have the power to obey God. The contradiction between subject and object is abolished and Christians experience kinship with God.[86] In this world, however, Christians are only witnesses to their existential fulfilment and share in the ambiguity and relativity of this world. What is new is that they now can perceive its relativity.[87] Since this world can never be a righteous place, all that is left for Christian life is to do penance and to change attitudes to accept the problems of this world in the light of eternity. The only possibility for true love, agape, in this world is to deny all things worldly.[88]

According to Nygren, Paul says that the Christian is transformed profoundly, when he/she is liberated from the destructive forces. In the last resort, they are incapable of harming him any more. However, it is characteristic of Christian life in this world, that Christians are still influenced by the destructive forces. This is how Nygren interprets the simul justus et peccator doctrine of

---

[84] For the discussion of ch 7, especially 7:13/14–25, see chapter one.

[85] Barth 1926 pp 9, 96 and 439.

[86] Barth 1926 p 192: "Die Gnade ist die Kraft des Gehorsams, weil und sofern sie die Kraft der Auferstehung ist, die Kraft der Erkenntnis, in der wir uns selbst erkennen als das Subjekt des *Futurum resurrectionis* . . ." See also pp 196f, 278f and p 281: "Dieser 'Geist der Sohnschaft', dieser neue Mensch, der nicht ich bin, ist mein unanschauliches existentielles Ich."

[87] Barth 1926 p 296: "Also unanschaulich herkommend vom Geiste Gottes geht der Mensch anschaulich ganz und gar hinein in eine unendliche Zweideutigkeit." See also pp 297, 415f and 449f.

[88] Barth 1926 p 362: "Die Kirche (. . .) wäre dann der Ort, wo im Unterschied zu allerlei andern Orten die angemessene (und nie ausgemessene!) *Distanz* gegenüber dem Allerhöchsten und Allertiefsten wahrgenommen, geschaffen und gewahrt wird, . . ." and p 422: "Die primäre ethische Handlung ist ein ganz bestimmtes *Denken*. Buße heißt *Um*-Denken." See also pp 361 and 476f.

Luther on the basis of Romans.[89] Nevertheless, it is the ideal of Christian life not to give up and adjust to this world, but to be transformed in thought and deed, even if fulfilment still lies in the future.[90] This transformation is guided by the special Christian (or Pauline) ethics, characterized by agape.[91]

Cranfield, too, focuses on the present situation of the Christian. Justification has necessary moral implications, since the Christian has been liberated for, and made capable of, obedience.[92] Although Paul does not refer to it in Romans, he regards sanctification as "the natural sequel to justification and also the earthly road which leads to the heavenly glory."[93] Sanctification is a process which continues throughout the whole of the Christian's life, since he/she is never entirely free from sin in this world.[94] Sanctification is thus understood in primarily moral terms and there are strong links between obedience in the Christian life of the present and ultimate salvation.

Wilckens holds that Paul understands the atonement to have taken place in order to render righteousness effective as love.[95] Thus Christians can perform righteous works, which express their relationship to God and mark their loyalty to the covenant. They can obey God.[96] However, Wilckens also asserts that, according to Paul, Christians are still under attack from sin. The difference is that they can now differentiate between themselves and sin on the one hand and the fact that sin is no longer their ultimate fate on the other.[97] Salvation will eventually be brought to fulfilment and the Christians will obtain ultimate salvation.[98]

Thus, on this issue, the four interpreters can be graded according to a scale that stretches from a negative view of the effect of righteousness in Christian life in this world to a view that is fairly positive. First, Barth describes Christian

---

[89] Nygren 1944 p 302, 1952 p 295: "The Christian – in this present world: there we face the dualism and the tension in the Christian's status. As a Christian he belongs to Christ and lives his life 'in Christ'; but as one who belongs to the old aeon, he still lives 'in the flesh.' " See also 1944 pp 303–307, 314–316, 327f and 344, 1952 pp 296–300, 307–309, 320–322 and 338.

[90] Nygren 1944 pp 269f and 416f, 1952 pp 262f and 417f.

[91] Nygren 1944 pp 436–439, 1952 pp 437–440.

[92] Cranfield 1985 (1) p 295 on 6:1–23: "Paul is here concerned to insist that justification has inescapable moral implications, . . ." See also p 300 and 1986 (2) pp 593f. Cf p 861 (essays).

[93] Cranfield 1985 (1) p 433.

[94] Cranfield 1985 (1) p 327 and 1986 (2) pp 607 and 729.

[95] Wilckens 1978 (1) p 293: ". . .Gottes Gerechtigkeit besteht in seiner Gnade, weil sie mit seiner Liebe identisch geworden ist" and "Paulus meint vielmehr, daß der uns gegebene Geist in unseren Herzen die Liebe Gottes bezeugt (8,16) und wirksam werden läßt (Gal 5, 22)." See also 1982 (3) p 7.

[96] Wilckens 1980 (2) pp 20, 22 and 129. However, there is a tension between Wilckens' assertion of the transformation of the Christians and his warnings against its relevance for life in this world. See pp 70–73 (Zusammenfassung) and 77.

[97] Wilckens 1980 (2) pp 17–20.

[98] Wilckens 1978 (1) p 297: "Er gehört nun zu denen, die am Ende vor dem Zorngericht gerettet werden" and 1980 (2) p 158.

life in negative terms. The Christian does not belong to this world and should dissociate himself from it. Secondly, Nygren holds Paul to mean that the Christian belongs both to this world and to the kingdom of God. This dualism makes meaningful the struggle against the forces of destruction. Thirdly, Wilckens interprets Paul to mean that the Christian is transformed in this world and both can and must make it better. Cranfield shares the same optimistic view, but gives it still more weight by opening up the way at least for the righteous life of the Christian as a precondition of ultimate salvation.

Finally, let us turn to the interpretation of the relationship between eschatological fulfilment and present day reality in Romans. According to Barth, Paul says that this world is totally negated by the world to come. However, the kingdom of God is not the simple antithesis of this world, but the negation of the negation, the dialectical synthesis of this world and its negation.[99] God's reality is totally separated from this world. Although Christians still live in this world, they belong to the world to come.[100] Barth understands Paul to hold that Christianity is at bottom eschatology.[101] Barth has a futuristic understanding of Paul's view of eschatology.

Nygren asserts that Paul comprehends the new aeon primarily as a new state of being, which has far-reaching consequences for Christian life in this world.[102] Though this world and the world to come are two separate realities, the Christian belongs to both. Nygren does not see Paul as understanding the kingdom of God to be fully realized, but as also expecting salvation to be fulfilled in the future, after the day of judgment.[103] The eschatology in Romans is ultimately realized, though it still awaits its fulfilment, when Christians will belong only to the kingdom of God.

Cranfield thinks Paul interprets God's work in Christ mainly as an act of correction. What had gone wrong has now been put right.[104] Since the purpose of God's condemnation of sin was that the lives of Christians should be

---

[99] Barth 1926 pp 271–274, 313 and 465–467.

[100] This can be seen from the changed attitude of the Christians towards this world: they perceive its relativity. See Barth 1926 pp 398 and 460f. They are hereby brought into a new kind of pain and distress as a consequence of their new insights, see pp 284f and 374.

[101] Barth 1926 p 298: "Christentum, das nicht ganz und gar und restlos Eschatologie ist, hat mit Christus ganz und gar und restlos nichts zu tun."

[102] Nygren 1944 p 152, 1952 p 145: "Like God's wrath in the old aeon, so the righteousness of God in the new is in highest degree an active and effective entry of God, by which the whole existence and circumstance of man are affected." See also 1944 pp 17 and 416f, 1952 pp 9f and 417f.

[103] Nygren 1944 p 209, 1952 p 204: "He who believes in Christ is certainly saved now; but salvation is full and final only when one is delivered from the wrath to come. It is only then that Christ's work for us attains its fullness." See also 1944 pp 200 and 347–350, 1952 pp 194f and 341–344.

[104] Cranfield 1985 (1) pp 219f, where (for example) the law of faith is understood to mean the Old Testament law rightly understood. See also pp 223f.

made righteous, Paul thought the eschatological promises were already beginning to be fulfilled in the lives of the Christians.[105] The decisive act was already in the past, but there was also future fulfilment ahead. According to Cranfield, however, Paul stresses the importance of the time between now and the final resurrection and parousia as a time for people to hear the gospel.[106] Eschatology is thus realized, but still on its way to fulfilment.

God's sacrifice in Christ was the decisive turning point, according to Wilckens' interpretation. This presented the world to come as a reality for Christians here and now.[107] Although the last judgment and ultimate fulfilment are still to come, it is only a matter of the development of the present reality.[108] Wilckens interprets the eschatology as being largely realized and yet still on its way to fulfilment.

Thus, these four commentators also understand Romans differently on this issue. While Cranfield and Wilckens hold Paul to have a realized eschatology, Barth takes the contrary view. This world is to be negated and replaced by a new synthesis. Eschatology should be understood futuristically. Nygren's interpretation of Romans lies between the two. He stresses that the eschatology is both realized and not realized in the life of the Christian, who lives in both aeons.

4. Conclusions

What are the differences between the authors' interpretations of the answers to some theological questions which Paul puts in his Epistle to the Romans, i e the theological themes discussed in this analysis?

Let me start with the single point of agreement that I have found: all four authors agree that Paul believed that Man was justified by faith alone. Surprisingly, they all disagree as to how this was made possible according to Romans, that is, they disagree concerning the atonement.

A doctrine of atonement answers at least three questions: what caused the

---

[105] See the interpretation of 8:4, Cranfield 1985 (1) p 159: "... for it is abundantly clear that Paul did think that God's eschatological promises were already beginning to be fulfilled through the gospel in the lives of believers, both Jews and Gentiles." See also pp 383–385.

[106] Cranfield 1985 (1) p 89. See also p 419: "The full manifestation of our adoption is identical with the final resurrection of our bodies at the Parousia, ..." For the importance of the intervening period see Cranfield 1986 (2) pp 683f.

[107] Wilckens 1978 (1) pp 276–279 and 1982 (3) pp 74–76. Note the translation of 13:11a: "Und das (tut) in der Erkenntnis der (gegenwärtigen) Zeit, (nämlich) daß die Stunde schon da ist für euch, vom Schlaf aufzustehen."

[108] Wilckens 1982 (3) p 76: "Darin zeigt sich, daß die präsentische Eschatologie der Taufaussagen die Zukünftigkeit des Endheils selbst keineswegs etwa aufhebt" and 1980 (2) p 158. On the idea of the unity between Christian life in this world and the world to come see p 165, where Wilckens speaks of "die *Einheit* der Heilsgeschichte".

need for salvation? How did Jesus Christ bring salvation to Man? Why did God become a human being? It is possible from the different answers to characterize different types of doctrines of atonement.

Characteristic for Nygren's interpretation of the view of atonement is that it is based on the idea of the struggle between God and the destructive forces. This type of view of the atonement points in the direction of a dramatic doctrine of atonement.[109] The view found in Cranfield's commentary points in the direction of a penal doctrine of atonement. The penal doctrine is characterized by sin interpreted as transgression of God's inviolable law and Christ is said to take upon himself the punishment imposed for human sin. Wilckens' interpretation of the view of atonement given in Romans has been clarified as pointing in the direction of a special kind of satisfaction doctrine of atonement. Human sin violates not God's honour, as in Anselm, but God's covenant with Israel. According to this view, Israel ought to be punished, but since the transgression is so grave, this is impossible. God then renders satisfaction for the transgression himself. Wilckens holds that Paul sees all this in the cultic context. Christ is the atonement sacrifice, which restores the order of the covenant. I call the doctrine of atonement which Wilckens indicates a satisfaction doctrine of atonement in a cultic context.

The view of atonement found in Barth's interpretation of Paul does not point in the direction of the types of doctrines usually mentioned. Its starting point is the fundamental and insuperable difference between God on the one hand and the human world, the creation, on the other. This difference is overcome in Christ. The doctrine indicated by Barth I call a dialectic doctrine of atonement.

The four commentaries thus interpret Paul similarly in one respect and completely differently in another. Several similarities can, however, be found between Barth's and Nygren's commentaries on the one hand and those of Cranfield and Wilckens on the other.

Expressions are found both in Barth's and Nygren's commentaries which suggest that Paul holds God to be fundamentally different both from mankind and from this world. This is clear from what has just been observed concerning Barth. In Nygren's commentary this can be seen from the circumstance, for example, that God overcomes the four forces which characterize the life of this world in Christ. Barth and Nygren both hold that these are expressions of the view of God's fundamental character which makes God completely different, i e God's love, agape. Cranfield and Wilckens share the view that Paul understands the old covenant to refer primarily to God's covenant with

---

[109] In this section I make use of Richardson 1964 pp 96–113, although my terminology differs from his concerning the characterization of Nygren's type of doctrine. Richardson simply refers to this type as Aulén's theory.

Israel. Human sin expresses itself as disobedience against the law of the covenant. God's act of salvation in Christ is motivated by the circumstance that God is both benevolent and harsh at the same time, both righteous and loving.

Thus where Barth and Nygren refer in their interpretations to the fundamental difference between God and this world, Cranfield and Wilckens refer to human disobedience. Furthermore, when Barth and Nygren refer to the emphasis in Romans on God's all-embracing love, which triumphs over his wrath, Cranfield and Wilckens understand Paul to keep the dual picture of God and take this to motivate his view of atonement. Thus, while there is a kind of dualism concerning the ontology in Barth's and Nygren's interpretations of Romans, there is a kind of dualism concerning the image of God in the commentaries of Cranfield and Wilckens.

The fundamental distance between God's reality and that of this world is also expressed in Barth's and Nygren's commentaries when human beings are said to be declared righteous in Romans. The change is not something which is observable in this world, or at least not primarily. Cranfield's and Wilckens' commentaries rather understand Paul to view this world as being corrected or repaired by God's act in Christ. This world is also the locus of God's reality. Human beings are made righteous in this life and they move on towards fulfilment. Thus, the commentaries all show a clear consistency in the interpretation of the issues relating to the third article of faith. While Barth and Nygren have (various degrees of) rather negative interpretations of the possibilities of Christian life in this world, Cranfield and Wilckens are more optimistic. As a result, Barth and Nygren put forward a futuristic eschatology, while Cranfield and Wilckens, although not denying that fulfilment lies in the future, rather put forth a realized eschatology.

This chapter leaves many questions to be answered: how can there be total agreement on the issue of justification by faith and at the same time four different doctrines of atonement? How are we to explain the similarities between Barth's and Nygren's interpretations of Paul on the one hand and those of Cranfield and Wilckens on the other? The results in this chapter do not however coincide with those in chapter one, where many similarities were found, for example between the commentaries of Nygren and Cranfield. The analysis so far points in two different directions. How can this be explained? Before attempting in chapters four, five and six, to find answers to these questions I would like to clarify the differences between the commentators' interpretations of Romans in still one more respect, that is, concerning their general remarks on Paul's Epistle to the Romans.

Chapter Three

General Remarks on Romans

Who was Paul? Was he a devout servant of his God or was he perhaps just out for power?[1] Was he a scholarly theologian or a man of action who dealt in his letters with the problems that currently engaged him? And what about the Romans? Were they threatened by a serious split or did they constitute a strategic point of departure for Paul's missionary work to whom Paul was anxious to introduce himself? What is the real purpose of Romans? What is its primary thesis? Answering these questions is also part of the process of interpreting Romans, although they are not interpretation problems in the strict sense. The answers to these questions are however necessary for the interpretation of the text. For this reason, I call the questions in this chapter not problems of interpretation, but analysis questions and the answers not interpretations, but general remarks.

The issues raised here are usually dealt with in the commentaries' introductory remarks; but since I have found that they are not restricted only to the introductions, I have chosen to call them general remarks. Good reasons could be given for starting with these general remarks instead of saving them till the end of part one. However I have preferred to start with the detail, so as not to give the impression that the thematic and detail levels are only consequences of the general, which is not the case. This order makes it easier to show how complicated the picture actually is. Furthermore, the focus of this study lies in the interpretation of the text of Romans and the strict interpretation problems ought therefore to be analysed first. By the end of chapter three we shall have achieved an overall picture of the four interpretations by Barth, Nygren, Cranfield and Wilckens and of the differences between them.

The questions which concern the general remarks on this epistle are of basically two types: they either concern the historical context (the situation of Paul and of the Roman congregation) or the content (theme) of the epistle.[2]

---

[1] Proposed by Shaw 1982 pp 138–140: Paul wants to establish his authority. The letter is polemical and aggressive.

[2] "Theme" should here be understood to refer to the theme of the content of Romans as presented by the commentators. It is not to be understood in any qualified sense, presupposing that Romans is a systematic exposition of a single theme. It is to be understood in the simple sense that every text is about something and this something is the theme of the text. Of course more than one theme is worked out in a text. What I am looking for here is the principal theme of Romans.

Questions concerning the purpose and character of Romans lie somewhere in between. I have chosen to include these questions in the latter group.

I have chosen to deal with the general remarks on the epistle in the following order:

1. The apostle Paul.
2. The Romans and Paul's opponents.
3. The purpose and character of Romans.
4. The theme of Romans.

I do not propose to pay any particular attention to questions concerning the authenticity of Romans or the date and place of its writing. Its authenticity is hardly under dispute. I disregard the text-critical problems of ch 16, which are of minor importance to this study and these authors.[3] There is also general agreement on the date and place of the writing of Romans. Romans is held to be written in Corinth, during Paul's three-month stay in Greece, referred to in Acts 20:2–3. It is also generally held that Romans was written after Galatians, although the absolute dating of the epistle is less certain. The four commentaries dealt with in this study all agree with this view. Although Barth and Nygren only touch upon these matters, they do not refute these historical results.[4]

1. The apostle Paul

Paul offers short presentations of himself in 1:1, 1:5 and 15:15b–20.[5] He can be characterized in many ways. He was a Christian apostle of Jewish origin, born in a Hellenistic environment. Different pictures emerge of Paul, depending on where one places the emphasis and how one understands these different aspects of Paul the person. How do Barth, Nygren, Cranfield and Wilckens describe Paul's persona, as a Christian apostle of Jewish origin?

First, these authors all agree that Paul had a special mission to the Gentiles. This is one of his prime reasons for writing to the congregation in Rome.[6] Wilckens gives prominence to the circumstance that Paul had to fight for his mission to be acknowledged, as can also be seen from Galatians. At

---

[3] Cf Barth 1926 pp 506–508, Nygren 1944 pp 455f, 1952 pp 456f, Cranfield 1985 (1) pp 5–11 and Wilckens 1978 (1) p 27.

[4] Cranfield 1985 (1) pp 2 and 12–16 and Wilckens 1978 (1) pp 27 and 44. Wilckens particularly stresses the close relation between Romans and Galatians both in time and content, pp 47f. Some of Barth's comments on the authenticity, date and place of writing are found in Barth 1926 pp 483 and 519. See also Nygren 1944 pp 12f and 456, 1952 pp 5f and 457.

[5] The discussion of Paul's relation to 7:7–25 is not dealt with here; see chapter one.

[6] Barth 1926 pp 513f, Nygren 1944 pp 71f and 453f, 1952 pp 63f and 454f, Cranfield 1986 (2) pp 763f and Wilckens 1978 (1) pp 62f.

the same time Paul was afraid the church might split, according to Wilckens.[7]

Secondly, Paul's Jewish origins are seen as important to a proper understanding of him. It is striking how different points of departure lend different meanings to this fact. Led by the use of the word ἀφωρισμένος in the first verse, possibly alluding to the word Pharisee, meaning someone set apart for God, Barth holds that Paul was a Pharisee, although unique.[8] Paul illustrates God's interaction with the world, the double predestination. Saul was rejected and wiped out, Paul is his new existence before God.[9] The difference between Saul and Paul is so great, that one might say that Barth holds Paul to be no longer a Jew – in the religious sense, that is. Nygren also takes his departure in the literal meaning of ἀφωρισμένος and very much shares Barth's view. Paul had set himself apart for the law, and now God has set Paul apart for something new and wholly different.[10] Nygren also thinks that Paul had a special competence, since he knew the two alternative ways to salvation.[11] Cranfield is critical of interpretations of ἀφωρισμένος which primarily indicate the setting-apart of Paul from something, rather than his setting-apart for the gospel. Cranfield also stresses the importance of the Old Testament background for the understanding of the gospel. Cranfield thus understands Paul's Jewish background as less in contrast to his present state.[12] This is why Paul is concerned in Romans with the correct interpretation of the Old Testament.[13] Wilckens takes a similar view of Paul's Jewish origins, but brings out a feature of Hellenistic Judaism (i e a branch of Judaism by the time of Paul, not just Judaism outside Palestine) not indicated by Cranfield: their apocalyptic notions. Not surprisingly, Wilckens takes many of his sources of comparison from the apocalyptic sources.[14]

Thus, these interpreters all agree that Paul had a special mission to the Gentiles; but they disagree concerning the implications of his Jewish origins. Barth and Nygren stress the contrast between the former Jew and the Christian apostle, while Cranfield and Wilckens see Paul's Christian mission less in contrast to his Jewish background. They point rather to Paul's reliance on Jewish sources for his thinking.

---

[7] Wilckens 1978 (1) pp 43–48 and 1982 (3) pp 128–130.
[8] Barth 1926 pp 3f.
[9] Barth 1926 pp 128f. See further below on 4. The theme of Romans.
[10] Nygren 1944 pp 52f, 1952 pp 45f.
[11] Nygren 1944 pp 18f, 1952 pp 11f.
[12] Cranfield 1985 (1) pp 53–55, including notes.
[13] Cranfield 1985 (1) pp 56f and 1986 (2) pp 445f. For the application see e g 1985 (1) p 227.
[14] Wilckens 1978 (1) pp 221 (excursus) and 96–100 and Wilckens 1980 (2) pp 147f, especially the notes, and p 183. The idea of Paul as a Greek philosopher, or at least greatly influenced by Greek philosophy, is not put forward by any of these authors. This view was firmly stated by many liberal theologians, such as Adolf von Harnack, Harnack 1927 pp 111f.

2. The Romans and Paul's opponents

The recipients of this epistle are the Christian congregation in Rome towards the end of the sixth decade of the first century. The interpreters differ concerning the importance of knowledge of the situation of the Roman congregation. However, they all have views about who comprise the cast of characters in Romans and what they represent. Furthermore, they differ as to who Paul's opponents are. The questions raised in this section are several: how important is knowledge of the situation of the Romans for the correct interpretation of the epistle? If it is important, what do we know about them? Who are the Jews and the Gentiles? How are Paul's opponents described and what is the main point of disagreement? What is the conflict between the strong and the weak about? Who are they? What does Paul's solution imply?

These commentaries agree that Paul is writing here to a congregation that he did not found and has never visited. The majority of its members are strangers to Paul.[15] Two different conclusions can be drawn from this: either the identity of the Roman congregation, its structure and problems, are of little or no interest for the understanding of the epistle, or, though Paul was not personally familiar with the Roman congregation, he had knowledge of its structure and problems and any interpretation ought to take their situation into account.

Although not taking much interest in the historical context of Romans, Barth and Nygren do not deny it. They think, rather, that the problems of Romans are general problems and that the answers given in Romans are therefore answers which can be applied to people today as well as throughout history.[16] They therefore give no account of the structure of the congregation in Rome.

Cranfield and Wilckens, on the other hand, give a lot of thought to describing the Roman congregation. The most interesting and controversial question in this area is what groups existed and what characterized them. In its simplest form this is a question of whether the Jewish or Gentile Christians were in the majority. Cranfield holds that both were large groups.[17] Wilckens is more specific. He identifies the Jewish Christians as former Hellenistic Jews, some with their origins in the group round Stephanos in Jerusalem, which was regarded as liberal. Contacts with Gentiles were frequent in Hellenistic Judaism and some of the Gentiles became proselytes and counted as Jews in religious terms. Other Gentiles did not wholly convert. They were called God-fearers and kept some of the Jewish laws, e g the food laws, but they were not cir-

---

[15] Barth 1926 pp 519f, Nygren 1944 p 455, 1952 p 456, Cranfield 1986 (2) pp 783, 794 and 817 (essays) and Wilckens 1978 (1) p 33.
[16] Barth 1926 pp xf, Nygren 1944 pp 12 and 14–16, 1952 pp 4f and 6–9.
[17] Cranfield 1985 (1) p 21.

cumcised and they were still thought of as Gentiles. The Christian congregation originated from these Roman Jews, who also converted many of the God-fearers to Christianity. New Gentiles also joined the congregation. Thus there were three major groups: former Jews, former God-fearers and other Gentiles. Both Wilckens and Cranfield assume that many Jewish Christians were forced to flee during Claudius' reign and had only just returned.[18]

Closely related to, and not always separated from, the question of the identity of the groups within the congregation, is the question of the identity of the Jews and the Gentiles. The answers which Barth, Nygren, Cranfield and Wilckens give once more convey the differences in their understanding of the importance of the historical context of Romans.

Barth states explicitly that the categories of Jews and Gentiles are not primarily to be understood as historical entities, but show the divine reality of the double predestination: God rejects those who thought they were closely related to God (the Jews) and accepts those who seemed to be completely outside God's dominion (the Gentiles). Barth here neglects the ethnic sense and stresses the religious sense. Jews lack and Gentiles enjoy the right relation to God. He therefore applies this distinction on the whole to the church.[19]

Nygren carefully expounds the conflict between Jews and Gentiles, in which Paul finds himself. Both are however seen as examples of one of the basic attitudes of human beings and their relation to God. Jews and Gentiles both belong to the old aeon; both are sinners and both condemned. "He who through faith is righteous" is their opposite, and belongs to the new aeon.[20] As both Barth and Nygren understand Paul, Jews and Gentiles on the one hand and Christians on the other are opposite categories. Barth even holds members of Christian communities to be Jews and Gentiles, since they are religious and do not live the existentially fulfilled life with God.

Cranfield and Wilckens take as their starting point the distinction between Jews, who belong to God's elect, and Gentiles, who are outside the covenant.[21] What then is the point of discussing God's covenant with Israel in the Epistle to the Romans? Cranfield and Wilckens hold that, according to Paul, the unbelief and ultimate fate of the Jews was a problem to the Christians, since it questioned the credibility of God. Cranfield believes that this problem was discussed by the Jewish and Gentile Christians in Rome, while Wilckens maintains that it was discussed with the synagogue. The Jew in

---

[18] Wilckens 1978 (1) pp 35–39 and Cranfield 1985 (1) p 18.
[19] Barth 1926 p 401 on 11:26a: "Sondern die Armut, die Blöße, die Blindheit, die Hoffnungslosigkeit der Heiden, sofern sie im Gegensatz zu der Fülle, Gesundheit, Sattheit und Gewißheit Israels *den* Menschen bedeutet, der in Christus aus Gnade erwählt ist, ist gemeint." See also pp 400, 347–351 and 321f on the application to the church.
[20] Nygren 1944 p 156, see also pp 155–157 and 124, 1952 p 149, see also pp 147f and 118.
[21] Cranfield 1985 (1) pp 176f and Wilckens 1978 (1) pp 84–86.

2:17, for example, who asks questions in 3:1–8 and elsewhere, is a Jew from the synagogue in Rome. However, according to both commentators, the conflict between Jews, Gentiles and Christians had repercussions also within the congregation.[22]

The question of the identity of Jews and Gentiles is closely related to the question of who Paul's opponents are. Paul's Epistle to the Romans is, if not polemical, at least apologetic. What is the main bone of contention and how are Paul's opponents more specifically described?

Barth maintains that Paul's opponents were examples of people searching for different kinds of human righteousness, which is opposed to God's. Characteristic of Barth's understanding of Romans is that he does not place Paul's opponents outside the church, but stresses instead the ambiguous character of all kinds of religion, including the church. Chs 9–11 and 12–15 are therefore closely interrelated. Since both passages discuss the problem of religion, they both discuss the problem of the church. Barth regards this not as a restricted problem of specific religious groups, but essentially a profoundly human problem.[23] The opponents of Paul have in common their failure to give sufficient consideration to the difference between God and Man.

According to Nygren the characteristic feature of Paul's opponents is their inability to grasp the idea of justification through faith without works, since they have not rightly understood God. This is the case of all non-Christian religions, but especially of the Jewish religion. Nygren apprehends the same view in later opponents such as Gnostics, Catholics and the Social Gospel movement.[24] Thus Paul's opponents can also be found within the visible church.

According to Cranfield, Paul is mainly opposed to the Jews, who have misunderstood the meaning of their own law. They have primarily misunderstood the law in not grasping that "It was to faith in Christ that the law was all along leading".[25] Thus, when trying to obey the law, the Jews were not wrong, but their endeavours were inadequate in the sight of God. This is why Paul can say both that the Jews have misunderstood the law and that they

---

[22] Cranfield 1985 (1) p 19 and 1986 (2) pp 466f n 7. Wilckens 1978 (1) pp 34f, 42, 46 and 1980 (2) pp 181–183.

[23] Barth 1926 p 328: "Die Gesamtheit derer, die 'aus Israel stammen', die wiederum nur die Repräsentanten aller derer sind, die betende Hände zu Gott erheben, sie stehen also unter der Krisis jener Doppelheit der Kirche, anders ausgedrückt: jener Doppelheit der Prädestination." Note that Israel here refers to all who pray as well as to the church. See also pp 346 and 380f.

[24] Nygren 1944 p 114, 1952 p 108: "It is not God who is revealed in the 'non-Christian religions' but the corruption of man; not God's truth but man's falsehood", 1944 p 378, 1952 p 376: "However much Israel strives after righteousness, she *cannot* attain to it, because she seeks it by way of the law" and 1944 pp 172f, 1952 pp 164f against Catholicism, 1944 pp 258f, 1952 p 251 against Gnosticism and 1944 p 427, 1952 p 427 against "the fanatical view which makes the gospel into a law for society."

[25] Cranfield 1986 (2) p 505, see also pp 508f.

possess the embodiment of knowledge and truth in the law.[26] Precisely what then did the Jews misunderstand? They thought that by obeying the law they could put God in their debt. It was this claim, not their endeavours per se, that were wrong.[27] Thus, according to Cranfield, Paul thinks this conflict impossible within the Christian congregation.

Wilckens pictures Paul's opponents with reference to the circumstances in which the Roman congregation was founded. The Jews of the synagogue were upset by two things: their righteousness was called in question and the Jewish Christians had abolished the important distinction between proselytes and God-fearers. A debate was taking place which was intensified by the return of the Jewish Christians after Claudius' death.[28] The problem is closely related to Paul's own status, which he knows was questioned as a result of his radical message concerning Jewish righteousness.[29] What then is wrong with the Jewish religion? The Jews' mistake is that they have not obeyed the law and are therefore not righteous, but condemned.[30] Thus neither Cranfield nor Wilckens understands Paul's opponents primarily as a category existing within the church. According to Wilckens, however, this conflict between Jews and Christians threatened to develop into a conflict within the church because of the Judaizers, Christians who were not clearly distinguished from Judaism. This was something which Paul feared could cause a rift in the church.[31]

As to the conflict between the weak and the strong in 14:1–15:13 several questions need to be answered: what is the conflict about? what is its deeper, more general meaning? what is the identity of the groups? what does Paul's solution imply?

According to Barth's understanding of Romans, the conflict is not connected with Mosaic law, but with two ways of living in (Christian) religion. The strong know that God will judge everything human and know therefore that one way of living is not more pleasing to God than another. This is the meaning of the double predestination, according to Barth. All that is human is condemned – and redeemed. However, the weak do not have this knowledge and hold their abstinence to be pleasing to God.[32] Barth firmly stresses the gener-

[26] Cranfield 1985 (1) pp 166f.
[27] Cranfield 1985 (1) p 170 and 1986 (2) pp 505 and 510.
[28] Wilckens 1978 (1) pp 18 and 35–39.
[29] Wilckens 1978 (1) pp 62f and 122f, especially n 268.
[30] Wilckens 1978 (1) pp 132f, where Wilckens comments on 2:13 and the difference between righteousness ἐκ πίστεως and righteousness ἐξ ἔργων νόμου: "Der Gegensatz zwischen beiden, (...) besteht vielmehr einzig darin, daß *Sünder* aufgrund des *Gesetzes* keinerlei Rechtfertigung zu erwarten haben, *eben weil* das Gesetz nur denjenigen als Gerechten dem Leben zuspricht, der es *getan* hat (10,5 vgl. Gal 3,12), jedoch unwiderruflich jeden dem Verderben zuspricht, 'der nicht bleibt in allem, was geschrieben ist im Buch des Gesetzes, um es zu tun' (Gal 3, 10)."
[31] Wilckens 1978 (1) pp 46 and 69f (Zusammenfassung), 1982 (3) pp 129f.
[32] The identity of the strong and the weak: Barth 1926 pp 491–493, the double predestination: p 487. See further below: 4. The theme of Romans.

al application of the problem: it concerns the human dilemma. This is also shown by the circumstance that not just Christians, but all kinds of idealists are included among the weak from "Orphiker" to "Freiluftidealisten".[33]

The meaning of Paul's solution is that although the strong are basically right, the double predestination makes it clear that there is no fundamental way in which the strong can be separated from the weak (seen by Barth as representing two opposite life-styles), since both are human: "Gerechtfertigt ist an sich weder unser Leben noch unser Sterben, weder unser Ja noch unser Nein und also, von diesen beiden Endpunkten allen menschlichen Tuns aus gesehen, weder unser präziser, noch unser freier Lebensversuch."[34] The election of God depends solely on God's grace.[35] Paul's solution thus implies God's rejection of every human way of life.

Nygren does not connect the conflict with the Mosaic law either. He believes the conflict concerns some kind of religiously motivated, though not Jewish, abstinence. The basic meaning of the conflict however relates to the unity of the congregation. The groups differ in degree of faith, but none takes the view that the Christian should obey the law. "When the issue was the Christian's freedom from the law, Paul was inflexible."[36] They disagree rather as to how much Christian freedom permits. Paul's solution has general application for the unity of the church. Although he agrees with the strong, Paul "... here contends for Christian freedom, for the right of both weak and strong."[37] Paul's solution is that Christian freedom must be handled carefully if unity is to be achieved.[38]

Cranfield differs from Barth and Nygren in understanding Paul to focus on the range of application of the Mosaic law. The weak understand obedience to the ceremonial laws to be "an integral element of their response of faith to Jesus Christ ..."[39] However, the weak are not Judaizers, holding their obedience to be a claim on God for righteousness.[40] The strong did not hold obedience to the ceremonial laws to be part of their Christian lives. Although this was a Roman conflict, it was not unique, but a common problem of the church at the time, and the distinction between weak and strong accords rather well with that between Jewish and Gentile Christians.[41] The deeper mean-

---

[33] Barth 1926 p 492: "Hier sehen wir hinter dem Gemüseesser von Rom das zahllose Volk der Orphiker, (...) Neupythagoräer, Therapeuten (...), die Täufer der Reformationszeit, die Abstinenten, Vegetarier und Freiluftidealisten der Gegenwart."

[34] Barth 1926 p 497, see also pp 487–490 and 498.

[35] Barth 1926 p 494: "Es gibt nur *einen* Vorsprung: die göttliche Erwählung ..." and p 497.

[36] Nygren 1944 p 441, 1952 p 442.

[37] Nygren 1944 p 443, 1952 p 444.

[38] Nygren 1944 pp 446f and 449f, 1952 pp 446f and 450f.

[39] Cranfield 1986 (2) p 697, see also p 696.

[40] Ibid.

[41] The identity of the strong: Cranfield 1986 (2) p 713, the common conflict: p 729 and Jewish and Gentile Christians: pp 740f.

ing of the conflict concerns the scope of Christian freedom.[42] It is serious, since, according to Cranfield's understanding of Romans, the freedom of the strong threatens the spiritual development of the weak. Cranfield holds this to be more than just a tragic event; "his salvation (is) put at risk".[43] Paul's solution is for the strong to renounce their freedom for the sake of the weak, so as not to jeopardize the weak's eternal fate.[44]

Wilckens agrees with Cranfield in that he holds that the conflict concerns the scope of application of the Mosaic law.[45] Wilckens' understanding, however, differs from Cranfield's in that he believes the conflict to have been caused by two Gentile Christian groups, those who were numbered among the God-fearers of the synagogue and those who were not. It was the God-fearers, who had once been excluded from full communion with the Jews by means of the law, who were most eager not to keep it as Christians, while the weak wanted to keep some of the Jewish ritual laws.[46] Nevertheless, the conflict was common in the first century and was also closely related to the problem of the relation between Jews and Gentiles, both within the Christian congregations and between the religious groups.[47] The conflict also has a deeper meaning in that the unity of the congregation (and other congregations) is threatened by the different conclusions people drew from their faith.[48] Paul's solution is to plead for unity as the characteristic and prime consequence of Christian faith. "Gegenseitiges konkretes Annehmen ist das Grundgesetz alles christlichen Zusammenlebens."[49] As Wilckens understands Paul, this concerns the entire church.[50]

Thus, while Cranfield and Wilckens hold knowledge of the Roman congregation to be important for the correct interpretation of Romans, Barth and Nygren focus on the epistle's general meaning. Cranfield and Wilckens however differ in their descriptions of the situation.

Their different attitudes towards historical knowledge are reflected in the interpreters' descriptions of the identity of the Jews and the Gentiles. Barth and Nygren describe them as primarily religious categories, while Cranfield and Wilckens describe them primarily as ethnic groups. Another difference is that Barth and Nygren view both groups in sharp contradistinction to Christ-

---

[42] Cranfield 1986 (2) pp 697f.
[43] Cranfield 1986 (2) p 714. See also pp 717 and 723.
[44] Cranfield 1986 (2) pp 725f and 730f.
[45] Wilckens 1978 (1) pp 39f and 1982 (3) p 79.
[46] Wilckens 1978 (1) pp 39–41 and 1982 (3) p 87 (Zusammenfassung).
[47] Wilckens 1978 (1) p 41, 1982 (3) pp 83 and 107 on 15:7–9a: "Sieht man so den Duktus der Gedankenführung in VV 7–9a, dann ist zunächst klar, daß Paulus den Konflikt zwischen den 'Starken' und 'Schwachen' in Rom im Gesamthorizont des heilsgeschichtlichen Verhältnisses zwischen Israel und den Heiden sieht."
[48] Wilckens 1982 (3) pp 81f.
[49] Wilckens 1982 (3) p 105. See also pp 84f, 93 and 100f.
[50] Wilckens 1982 (3) pp 94f. See also the application for today pp 99f (Zusammenfassung).

ianity, while Cranfield and Wilckens focus on the problematic relation between Jews and Christians and the consequences of the conflicts between Jews and Gentiles for the Christian congregations (the relation between Jewish and Gentile Christians). Wilckens even holds that Paul is conducting a dialogue with a Jew from the synagogue. As for Paul's opponents, Cranfield and Wilckens identify them as the Jews, while Barth and Nygren, in accordance with their wider understanding of the identity of the Jewish people, hold them to be people also of other religions and other views of Christianity (Nygren) and humanity, in the sense that Paul is concerned with the basic human dilemma (Barth). However, Cranfield and Wilckens differ on what is wrong with Jewish religion. While Cranfield says that the Jews did not understand that Christ represented the deeper meaning of the law, Wilckens holds that they were rejected because they actually broke the law.

On the conflict between the strong and the weak, Cranfield and Wilckens believe it concerns the scope of application of the Mosaic law, while Barth and Nygren reject this. This difference is reflected in the four commentaries' understandings of the identity of the conflicting groups. Neither Cranfield nor Wilckens identifies the groups as Jewish and Gentile Christians, but both point in that direction. Barth and Nygren focus on groups with no ethnic connection. As to the deeper meaning and the solution of the problem, Nygren and Wilckens however both understand the problem to deal basically with the unity of the community and agree that the solution is not to give up this unity, which is the basic characteristic of faith. According to Barth, Paul's solution to the human dilemma is constantly to reinforce the meaning of the double predestination, that everything human is rejected. Cranfield sees the deeper meaning of the problem as the danger that the strong Christians pose for the weak. The risk is so grave that the strong are called upon to renounce their freedom. Barth's and Cranfield's understandings of the solution put forward by Paul are thus more firmly linked to the problem under discussion, while Nygren's and Wilckens' commentaries focus on a more fundamental problem of which the problem under discussion functions as an illustration.

3. The purpose and character of Romans

So far, the analysis of this chapter has shown that there are many differences between Barth's and Nygren's commentaries on the one hand and those of Cranfield and Wilckens on the other. These can be traced back to the different degree of interest they evince in the situation of the Roman congregation, in its turn traceable to their different views concerning Paul's purposes in writing Romans. To clarify the alternatives one might put it like this: did Paul set out to clear up some theological questions, regardless of the special circumstances prevailing at the time, or did he set out to solve some concrete problems – his own, the Romans' or those of the early church? Closely related to this is the question of the character of Romans. Is it really a letter or is it a general theological essay?

Barth, Nygren, Cranfield and Wilckens agree that Paul's purpose was to present his gospel; but what was Paul's motivation in presenting it? Barth and Nygren take Paul's primary motive to be his belief that this was his vocation and his responsibility. What he wanted to do was to discuss some central theological issues. According to Barth, these were not specific for his time. The historical circumstances are therefore not important for the interpretation of Romans.[51] Nygren holds Paul to rely less on the problems of the recipients than in the other epistles, and Romans therefore has "a uniquely objective character".[52] Here "the gospel speaks, more clearly than anywhere else, against the law as a background."[53] Barth and Nygren thus take Paul's purpose to be the presentation of his gospel, motivated by his vocation.

Cranfield and Wilckens agree that Paul's primary purpose was to present his gospel, but disagree concerning his motives. Cranfield focuses on Paul's travel and missionary plans. He seeks to introduce himself by giving a summary of his gospel, thereby ensuring himself of support. For this reason he is also eager to clear up misunderstandings about himself among the Jewish Christians in Rome.[54] Wilckens focuses on Paul's concern for the relations between Jewish and Gentile Christians in the early church. Paul wanted to prevent the split that threatened the church, and was partly the result of his own theology. In a wider context this conflict also bore on the relation between Jews and Gentiles and ultimate salvation.[55] Connected with this is his defence against allegations that he was a pseudo-apostle.[56]

Surprisingly, perhaps, all four agree that Romans differs from the rest of Paul's epistles in being less influenced by the problems of Paul himself, or of the different congregations. Barth calls it a theological and philosophical diatribe and Wilckens holds it to be Paul's testament, both as regards theology

---

[51] Barth 1926 pp 3f on Paul's special call, p 517, where Barth asserts that Paul's gospel is not human, since "er sein Evangelium von keinem Menschen gelernt noch empfangen habe (Gal. 1,11–12)" and p xiv concerning his own interpretation: "Ist sie falsch, hat Paulus wirklich von etwas anderem geredet als von der permanenten Krisis von Zeit und Ewigkeit, nun, dann werde ich mich ja im Verlauf seines Textes selbst *ad absurdum* führen."

[52] Nygren 1944 p 12, 1952 p 5.

[53] Nygren 1944 p 16, 1952 p 9. See also 1944 p 50, 1952 p 43.

[54] Cranfield 1986 (2) pp 815–818 (essays). See also 1985 (1) pp 22f.

[55] Wilckens 1978 (1) p 47. See also p 48: "Aus der Polemik des Galaterbriefs ist im Römerbrief eine umfassende Apologie geworden, die über die örtlich-situationsbedingte Bedeutung des galatischen Konflikts hinaus eine gesamtkirchlich-allgemeine Bedeutung gewonnen hat." Further pp 69f (Zusammenfassung), 1980 (2) pp 181–183, 265 (Zusammenfassung) and 1982 (3) p 116 on the salvation-historical context.

[56] Wilckens 1978 (1) pp 43–46 and 1982 (3) pp 130f (Zusammenfassung).

and church politics. Nygren and Cranfield both esteem Romans very high, judging it the clearest exposition of the gospel in the New Testament.[57] But none of these commentators denies that it is also a real letter. Possibly they would agree with Norman Perrin in describing it as a letter-essay.[58]

Thus, Barth and Nygren hold that Paul's purpose was to clear up some theological questions, regardless of the special circumstances prevailing at the time, and they agree as to his motivation. Cranfield and Wilckens stress the concrete situation of the Romans and the whole church at the time, although they view it in different ways. Cranfield focuses on Paul's missionary plans, while Wilckens points to the threatened split in the church. All four commentators however agree that Paul's epistle to the Romans is a letter-essay.

4. The theme of Romans

What is Romans about? This is the question of the theme of Romans. The question can be understood in two ways. It can be understood to concern the content of Romans or a specific verse or set of verses, which are regarded as the theme, i e a question of the disposition of Romans. I focus on the content sense of the question, but will show that this coincides with the disposition sense in these commentaries. What is the theme of Romans? How should it be interpreted?[59] How is it developed in the epistle as a whole?

Barth, Nygren, Cranfield and Wilckens all agree that the theme of Romans is contained in 1:16–17, although the exact limits vary a little.[60] The next section in which the theme of Romans is found is given, with minor variations, as Romans 3:21–26. Although not explicitly stated in Barth's and Nygren's commentaries, it is clear that they view this passage as expressing the same ideas as are contained in 1:16–17.[61]

[57] Barth 1926 p 488. Nygren 1944 p 16, 1952 pp 8f, Cranfield 1985 (1) p 31 and Wilckens 1978 (1) pp 48f.

[58] Barth 1926 pp 519f, Nygren 1944 p 15, 1952 pp 7f, Cranfield 1985 (1) p 11, Wilckens 1978(1) pp 15 and 27f and Perrin and Duling 1982 p 188, where also Stirewalt 1977 pp 176f is referred to.

[59] A problem of interpretation is raised by the first analysis question. This shows how closely the general remarks and the problems of interpretation are interrelated.

[60] Barth 1926 p 10: "Die Sache. 1,16–17", Nygren 1944 p 73, 1952 p 65: "The Theme of the Epistle 'He Who through Faith is Righteous Shall Live'. 1:16–17", Cranfield 1985 (1) p 87: "The Theme of the Epistle is Stated. (1.16b–17)" and Wilckens 1978 (1) p 77, although he does not set a sharp limit between 1:16–17 and the preceding verses: "Daran schließt sich eine grundsätzliche Begründung seines Kommens (VV 14f) und eine ebenso grundsätzliche Charakterisierung des Evangeliums (VV 16f), die zugleich das Thema der gesamten folgenden Erörterungen des Briefkorpus (1,18–11,36) darstellt."

[61] Barth 1926 pp 66–68, cf pp 13–15, Nygren 1944 pp 152f, 1952 pp 145f. Note that Nygren takes 3:21–31 as a unit. Cf 1944 p 80, 1952 p 72. Nygren also stresses that the theme is given already in 1:4 and 1:7, indicating that Paul's epistle is a strict unity from the very beginning, Nygren 1944 pp 59 and 66, 1952 pp 51f and 58. Cranfield 1985 (1) p 199 on 3:21–26: "This short section is, as has already been indicated, the centre and heart of the main division to which it belongs. We may go farther and say that it is the centre and heart of the whole of Rom 1.16b–15.13." Wilckens 1978 (1) p 182, where 3:21–26 is called "Die These".

In its most general form, this theme is expressed by the four interpreters in similar terms: Man has been made righteous through faith in God's act in Christ.[62] These commentators thus agree that Paul's message in Romans is justification through faith. But what does the message mean? How should it be clarified? The authors' answers to those questions make it clear that they are not in full agreement after all.

Barth states that Paul has another way of expressing the idea of justification through faith, that is, by means of the idea of the double predestination, which can be summed up thus: all men are subject to the judgment of God and all are objects of God's mercy. In the act of faith men can perceive God's mercy beyond his judgment. The key to clarification of the meaning of Romans is to be found in 11:32.[63]

Nygren holds that underlying Paul's view of justification is the hidden pattern special to Paul, which must be found if the epistle is to be understood. It is expressed in 5:12–21: "all that we call life (. . .) lies under the dominion of death" and "the new age, the age of life, has burst upon us."[64] The righteousness of faith is thus something totally different from previous attempts at righteousness and must be understood through the idea of the two aeons.

According to Cranfield, Paul's view of justification needs to be understood against the Old Testament background. From this it is clear that God had to act in such a way as to remain righteous at the same time as human beings were held morally accountable.[65]

Wilckens stresses that in this epistle Paul expounds the gospel with partic-

---

[62] Barth 1926 p 17 on 1:17: "Wo die Treue Gottes dem Glauben des Menschen begegnet, da enthüllt sich seine Gerechtigkeit. Da wird der Gerechte leben. Das ist die Sache, um die es im Römerbrief geht." Nygren 1944 pp 84f, 1952 p 76: "In summary fashion we could say, 'the righteousness of God' is a righteousness originating in God, prepared by God, revealed in the gospel and therein offered to us. It is the righteousness of the new age. In Christ it has come to us, and he who through faith belongs to Him has it as his righteousness." Cranfield 1985 (1) p 100 on the sense of 1:17a: "For in it (i. e. in the gospel as it is being preached) a righteous status which is God's gift is being revealed (and so offered to men) – a righteous status which is altogether by faith." Wilckens 1978 (1) p 89 on the meaning of the thesis in 1:17 in contrast to other opinions: "Nicht der Glaube *als solcher*, sondern der Glaube an den gekreuzigten *Christus* als den Grund aller Gerechtigkeit vor Gott, der Glaube an Gott, der den Gottlosen rechtfertigt (4,5), tritt der jüdischen These der Werk-Gerechtigkeit entgegen."
[63] Barth 1926 p 407, where Barth states that this verse is "das Kriterium der *doppelten Prädestination*". Cf p 13: "Gerade weil Gottes Nein! ganz ist, ist es auch sein Ja!" and pp 67–70 for the expression of the same idea.
[64] Nygren 1944 pp 29f, 1952 pp 22f and 1944 p 33, 1952 p 26: "If one would understand what Paul has to say in this epistle, he must from the start take seriously this affirmation about the two aeons." Cf 1944 pp 80f, 1952 pp 72f.
[65] Cranfield 1985 (1) p 200: " . . .whereas forgiveness on cheaper terms would have meant God's abandonment of His faithful love for man and the annihilation of man's real dignity as His morally accountable creature," God's costly forgiveness "is altogether worthy of the righteous, loving, faithful God, who does not insult or mock His creature man by pretending that his sin does not matter, but rather Himself bears the full cost of forgiving it righteously–lovingly." See also p 89 and 1986 (2) pp 445f for the Old Testament background of the theme.

ular reference to the inclusion of all – Jews and Gentiles, different groups of Gentile Christians, and Jewish Christians. The point is that all alike are objects of God's wrath and mercy and all form part of God's plan. Both judgment and justification by faith are universal in scope.[66]

It is obvious that these themes are reflected all through the commentaries. Although Nygren's and Cranfield's headings to chs 1:18–4:25 are very similar, the minor differences between them reveal their different elaborations of the theme:

Nygren: "He Who through Faith Is Righteous"
Cranfield: "The Revelation of the Righteousness which is From God by Faith Alone – 'He Who is Righteous by Faith' Expounded"

As we have seen, Nygren emphasises that the righteousness of faith is opposed to the righteousness of the old aeon and the words through faith are stressed by the sentence order. Cranfield, who gives the theme a moral touch, stresses the word righteous instead. This is still more obvious in Cranfield's heading to 12:1–15:13: "The Obedience to which Those Who are Righteous by Faith are Called".[67]

Most commentators have difficulty relating chs 9–11 and 12–15:13 to chs 1–8. The discussion of this rejection of the Jews occurs somewhat abruptly in chs 9–11 and the parenesis of Paul is, as usual, not quite clearly related to the main part of chs 1–8. However, the themes suggested by the commentators solve this problem.

According to Barth, chs 9–11 are about the church under the double predestination. The church is an ambiguous fact; it wants to be close to God, but reveals human enmity towards God.[68] Nygren, Cranfield and Wilckens all understand Paul to have written chs 9–11 in order to show that the new covenant which has come through Christ in fact accords with the promises of the old covenant, although Nygren points to the limitation of the old covenant and Cranfield and Wilckens to its endurance. According to Nygren, chs 9–11 show that the drama of salvation has taken a new course in the new covenant and therefore "Israel must first be cast down from her self-confidence."[69] Cranfield holds that since the Old Testament references are so clear already in the theme as it is expressed in 1:16b–17, it "requires the inclusion in the epistle of a discussion of the relation of the nation of Israel to the gospel."[70]

[66] Wilckens 1978 (1) pp 46, 131f, 250f (Zusammenfassung), 1980 (2) pp 259f and 1982 (3) pp 79f and 109 (Zusammenfassung).
[67] Cranfield 1986 (2) p 592, cf Nygren 1944 p 411, 1952 p 411: "The Life of Him Who through Faith Is Righteous."
[68] Barth 1926 pp 317 and 403–405. For explicit references to the idea of predestination see pp 334, 337 and 369.
[69] Nygren 1944 p 409, 1952 p 407, cf 1944 pp 360 and 362, 1952 pp 357 and 359f.
[70] Cranfield 1986 (2) p 446, see also pp 445–448.

Wilckens holds the meaning of chs 9–11 to be that of removing the misconception that there was a break between the two covenants, because then there would be no basis for the universal church comprising both Jews and Gentiles.[71]

The characterizations of the parenesis of 12:1–15:13 differ significantly from each other. Barth here understands Paul to be answering the question how it is possible to remain a Christian in this world, aware of God's judgment of this world and still a part of it.[72] Nygren understands Paul to be giving advice to the Christian on how to handle the fact that he is actually living in both the old aeon and the new.[73] Cranfield understands this section to be about Christian sanctification.[74] According to Wilckens, Paul is here once more expounding his gospel of unity and exhorting the Romans to live in accordance with it.[75]

Thus, though all agree that the theme is that Man has been made righteous through faith in God's act in Christ, they differ concerning its interpretation. Barth finds the key in the idea of the double predestination and Nygren in the idea of the two aeons. Cranfield finds it in the Old Testament background and the moral relation between God and Man and Wilckens in the fundamental call for unity. When examined more closely, their interpretations of the theme of Romans differ considerably and this analysis showed that these differences are found throughout the commentaries.

5. Conclusions

In this chapter we have seen once more that many differences exist between Barth's and Nygren's commentaries on the one hand and Cranfield's and Wilckens' on the other. These differences are very apparent in the answers they give concerning the importance of knowledge of the situation of the Roman congregation for a correct interpretation of Romans. Barth and Nygren hold it to be of no importance, while Cranfield and Wilckens believe it is important. This difference can be described as a difference in attitude towards the historical aspect of the general remarks. In Cranfield's and Wilckens'

---

[71] Wilckens 1980 (2) pp 181f.

[72] Barth 1926 pp 416f and 487f.

[73] Nygren 1944 pp 411–413, 1952 pp 411–413. N b the following key sentence from the Swedish has been omitted in the English translation p 412: "Detta den nya äonens liv har den kristne att leva mitt i den gamla äonen med dess ordningar;" My translation: "The Christian has to live this life of the new aeon in the very midst of the old aeon and its conditions."

[74] Cranfield 1986 (2) pp 592–594.

[75] Wilckens 1982 (3) pp 84f and 106: "Paulus will also sagen: Christus hat die Christen in Rom allesamt angenommen, die 'Schwachen' wie die 'Starken'. Denn durch ihn, in seinem Werk als ganzem, hat Gott allen Menschen, Juden wie Heiden, Rettung und Heil geschaffen."

commentaries many of the answers given to questions concerning the general remarks have a clear historical basis, while many of Barth's and Nygren's answers have a more general sense not connected with the historical situation of either Paul or the Romans.[76] This difference between historical and general answers may be observed in several of the general remarks above: the description of Paul, the description of the Jews and the Gentiles and their relation to Christianity, the description of the opponents of Paul, the description of the conflict between the strong and the weak and the description of Paul's purpose. However, there are general remarks where this difference is not present at all: the description of the more profound problem of the strong and the weak and of Paul's solution to this problem, and the commentators' different interpretations of the theme of Romans. Thus, there is a difference between Barth's and Nygren's general answers and Cranfield's and Wilckens' historical answers, but this difference in no way accounts for all the general remarks.

If we look more closely at the general remarks where the differences between historical and general answers are clear, we find that this difference alone is inadequate to describe the differences between the commentaries. Barth's and Nygren's general and Cranfield's and Wilckens' historical answers cannot account for the differences in their descriptions of Paul's relation to the past, i e his Jewish origin. Nor can it account for the different descriptions they give of the relation between Judaism and Christianity. Whether Judaism is viewed in opposition to Christianity does not depend on whether the answers are given in historical categories or not, but on how these groups are described, historically and generally. Finally, this difference cannot adequately describe the different views of Paul's opponents. It is possible to see that the different descriptions of Paul's opponents are connected with the commentators' views of the theme of the epistle which do not relate to the historical or general answers of the commentators. Thus, the differences between historical and general answers apply primarily only to the general remarks on the concrete conflict of 14:1–15:13, the identity of the strong and the weak and Paul's purpose in writing the epistle. The difference is more complex concerning the other issues.

We can also conclude that no general remarks follow as a consequence from either the historical or the general type of answers. In the case of the general answers, this is quite natural, since generalizations always involve simplification and selection so that the opportunities for variation increase. Considering that historical facts are always ambiguous and that the historical

[76] I have avoided terms like "theological answers" or "doctrinal answers", which are too biased for my purpose. "General answers" here means answers unrelated to the historical situation of Paul or of the Romans. It should not be confused with "general remarks".

evidence concerning the situation of the Romans is scant, it is also evident that historical answers differ in content. However, this is not infrequently forgotten. This outcome of the study therefore serves as a reminder that historical answers can also vary.

PART II:
EXPLAINING THE DIFFERENCES

Chapter Four

The Kinds of Interpretations

In the preceding chapters I *described* the differences between the four commentators' interpretations of Paul's Epistle to the Romans on different levels. In chapter one I described their different interpretations of Romans 7, in chapter two their different interpretations of some theological themes and in chapter three, their different general remarks on Romans. In chapters four, five and six I shall consider whether these differences can be *explained* by reference to the different kinds of interpretations employed by the authors (chapter four), their different purposes in writing their commentaries (chapter five) and some of the different basic assumptions they make (chapter six).

In order to be able to examine the differences between the interpretations of Romans on the three levels, I focus on the commentators' arguments for their interpretations. Identification of seven different kinds of arguments and relation of them to a theory of interpretation enables me to classify and compare the authors' kinds of interpretations and thus find some explanations for why they interpret the same text in different ways. My analysis instrument will be presented below.

I have chosen a limited number of problems of interpretation and general remarks from chapters one, two and three for this analysis. From chapter one I selected the most discussed problem of interpretation, i e the problem of the identity of ἐγώ. From chapter two I selected one problem of interpretation from each section. The problems are central and the analysis produces a picture clear enough to give the reader an idea of the commentators' arguments for their interpretations of closely-related issues. From chapter three I also chose a problem from each section, although the opportunities for drawing conclusions as far as the other questions dealt with are concerned are more limited.

For each problem of interpretation and each question concerning the general remarks, a number of possible alternative interpretations and answers are given. Compared with the analyses in part one, the alternatives are simplified. Thereafter follows a characteristic and representative formulation of each commentator's interpretation or general remark whereby the differences between the commentaries become clear.

The differences are explained with reference to the different types of arguments and their content given in support of each interpretation and general remark. The arguments which I bring out are characteristic and representative of the commentaries. It should be noted that what are here termed arguments are not necessarily explicitly described as arguments in the commentaries. Commentaries by definition have a way of commenting rather than arguing. Identifying the arguments has been crucial to my analysis. These arguments nevertheless are clearly supported in the text of the commentaries and I refer to them in numerous quotations.

The analysis instrument in this chapter is based on the definition of interpretation given in the introduction. However, when reading the commentaries, I have found that there are several different kinds of interpretations. I propose here to distinguish between seven different kinds of interpretations. These provide a suitable analysis instrument for my purpose of examining whether some of the differences between the commentators' interpretations of Romans 7 and some theological themes, and their various general remarks on Romans, can be explained by the fact that they aim at different kinds of interpretations.

I distinguish between the different kinds of interpretations in terms of the interpretation process. First, let me define the process of interpretation. In order to interpret a statement A a set of alternatives B_1, B_2, B_3 ... which mean the same as A are listed and then the number of alternatives are reduced so as to exclude at least one. The different criteria by which one excludes or prefers one or more alternatives to at least one or more other alternatives indicate different kinds of interpretations. These are the seven kinds of interpretations found in the commentaries:

1) *Philological* interpretation:
   An interpretation B of a statement A is a philological interpretation if the number of alternative statements B_1 ... B_n is reduced by reference to grammar, syntax or the dictionary meaning of a word.

2) *Contextual* interpretation:
   An interpretation B of a statement A is a contextual interpretation if the number of alternative statements B_1 ... B_n is reduced by reference to the context. The context referred to is the literary context. Two distinctions can be made: firstly, between immediate (same section) or close context and sources judged relevant, but not found in Romans; and secondly, between reference to the content of the context, e g the theme, and reference to the structure of the context.

3) *Historical* interpretation:
   An interpretation B of a statement A is a historical interpretation if the number of alternative statements B_1 ... B_n is reduced by reference to historical knowledge, that is, to the historical or social circumstances of the text, its author and its recipients.

4) *Intentional* interpretation:

An interpretation B of a statement A is an intentional interpretation if the number of alternative statements $B_1 \ldots B_n$ is reduced by reference to the author's intention.

5) *Natural* interpretation:

An interpretation B of a statement A is a natural interpretation if the number of alternative statements $B_1 \ldots B_n$ is reduced by reference to common sense or to the view of the majority of scholars.

6) *Consistency* interpretation:

An interpretation B of a statement A is a consistency interpretation if the number of alternative statements $B_1 \ldots B_n$ is reduced by reference to the purpose of rendering the text as consistent as possible. An interpretation of a statement is consistent when it renders the text as a whole free from logical contradictions.[1]

7) *Constructive* interpretation:

An interpretation B of a statement A is a constructive interpretation if the number of alternative statements $B_1 \ldots B_n$ is reduced by reference to the circumstance that this interpretation B follows as a logical consequence from the text and from certain other assumptions. These other assumptions may be of different kinds. They may be anthropological, ontological, philosophical or theological assumptions. These are theoretical assumptions which share the characteristic that they are not found in the text of Romans, but are introduced by the interpreter in order to obtain a better understanding of the statement interpreted.

My definitions of the different kinds of interpretations give rise to a problem of terminology. I shall refer, for example, both to philological interpretations and philological arguments. This is because the definitions of the different kinds of interpretations take as their starting point the interpretation process. An interpretation argued on the basis of philological arguments is called a philological interpretation etc.

A few comments need to be made. First, the contextual arguments differ from consistency arguments in that the contradictions found in the text are

---

[1] These kinds of interpretations have certain affinities with the reasonable interpretation in the introduction. However, a reasonable interpretation is a complex interpretation, which includes contextual, intentional, natural and consistency interpretations above. Furthermore, it is an evaluative interpretation, since it claims to be the most acceptable interpretation. In order to analyse the kinds of interpretations in the commentaries it has been thought better to keep the contextual, intentional, natural and consistency interpretations apart and leave the criterion of acceptability out. The consistency criterion of a reasonable interpretation is valuable, since one of the problems of the interpretation of Romans is that on several occasions Paul seems to contradict himself, cf e g 7:23 and 8:2. I have avoided calling this kind of interpretation consistent interpretation, since it could be taken to imply that the other interpretations are inconsistent.

dealt with in consistency interpretations, while in contextual interpretations the context is not viewed as problematic in that sense. Secondly, the natural interpretation based on an argument which relies on the authority of other scholars can be difficult to distinguish from references to other scholars as mere illustrations. This is also the case with other kinds of references, e g philological, contextual and constructive. These do not always constitute arguments for interpretation. Thirdly, the constructive arguments need not contain the interpreter's personal convictions. Fourthly, the distinction between constructive arguments and contextual arguments in particular can be difficult to make. No clear lines are drawn between text-internal and text-external references. It will be up to the reader to judge my classifications. However, it should be noted that the classification of an argument as part of a constructive interpretation is not a value-judgment, but simply a classification of an argument of a certain kind.

The seven kinds of interpretations differ from each other in several respects. The contextual and the intentional arguments, for example, bear different relations to the text. Contextual arguments refer to what the author has written and intentional arguments to the author himself. On the other hand the difference is less if contextual references are made, for example, to the Gospels. In such a case neither argument is directly related to the text of Romans. Although in some respects a weakness, the different characters of the interpretations is of great value when attempting to explain the different interpretations of the commentaries.

There is, however, one fundamental difference between these kinds of interpretations to which attention will be drawn. This is motivated by the fact that this study concentrates on the problem of the different biblical interpretations with special reference to systematic theology. There is a fundamental difference between kinds of interpretation 1–6 and kind 7. 1–6 focus on statements in their original context and are more internal to the text by comparison with the constructive interpretations (7). The latter add something new, something text-external to the process of interpretation, which is different from the references to the historical situation of the text and from the author's intention. While kind of interpretation 7 is constructive and creative in relation to the text, the other kinds of interpretations are *reconstructive*. When I refer to this distinction I shall therefore refer to *reconstructive* and *constructive* interpretations and arguments.

It is my impression that when exegetes speak of historical or intentional interpretation, they are often referring to the whole corpus of reconstructive interpretations.[2] As far as the constructive interpretations are concerned, it should be noted that they may be, but are not necessarily, a modern applica-

---

[2] Cf Dunn 1987 pp 12–14 and 20 and Fornberg 1981 pp 85–94.

tion of the statement. Ancient or modern philosophical or theological distinctions, for example, may be introduced to clarify the original meaning of a statement. Modern applications, however, are always constructive interpretations.[3]

1. The identity of ἐγώ

In chapter one we concluded that Barth, Nygren, Cranfield and Wilckens give different interpretations of the identity of ἐγώ in Romans 7:13/14–25. Using the analysis instrument, I propose to give an account of the arguments the interpreters advance for their interpretations. Let us first recall the different interpretations the commentators give:

Barth: ἐγώ is religious Man, who lives ante Christum, in this world.
Nygren: ἐγώ is the Christian living in both aeons.
Cranfield: ἐγώ is a mature Christian in this world.
Wilckens: ἐγώ is Man ante Christum, as viewed by the Christian.[4]

What kinds of arguments do the authors put forward in support of their interpretations? Do they pursue different kinds of interpretations?

Barth gives arguments of three kinds: contextual, natural and constructive. The contextual arguments are of two kinds, referring both to the immediate context and to the corpus paulinum, other New Testament passages and some Old Testament passages. However, it is often not entirely clear how these contextual references relate to the interpretation of the identity of ἐγώ. Some are less arguments than hints and notes.[5]

The natural arguments refer primarily to Calvin, Kierkegaard and Luther. Barth holds the view of religion to be supported by these three authorities. He holds that by religion Paul means "die Religion des 39. Psalms, Hiobs, Luthers und Kierkegaards . . ."[6]

Barth's first constructive argument is the theological argument of his view of religion. Of 7:21 Barth writes "Ein religiöser Mensch sein heißt ein zerris-

---

[3] Cf Stendahl 1962 pp 419f, where he makes the distinction between what the text *meant* and what it *means*.

[4] Cf chapter one: 1. Anthropology and the identity of ἐγώ.

[5] Barth makes frequent references to other parts of Romans, see e g Barth 1926 pp 245f, where he argues for his interpretation of 7:18–20 as part of the insight of the religious human being referring to 3:1–20 and 7:14. Mk 10:18 is referred to in the same passage in support of the rather pessimistic view of the religious human being, p 246. See also p 242, where reference is made to Lk 5:8. References to the corpus paulinum can be seen for example at p 242, where Eph 3:1, 4:1, 2 Tim 1:18 and Philem 1:9 are cited in support of the idea that human beings are necessarily religious. Jer 20:7 is cited on the same page.

[6] Barth 1926 p 240. The view of religion is also supported by a quotation of Calvin p 251.

sener, ein unharmonischer, ein unfriedlicher Mensch sein."[7] This corresponds to the very first sentence of Barth's commentary to 7:14–25 "Der Sinn der Religion ist der Erweis der Macht, mit der die Sünde diesen Menschen in dieser Welt beherrscht: auch der religiöse Mensch ist Sünder, gerade er, gerade er als solcher!"[8] Barth has a negative view of religion, and this enables him to interpret Romans 7 as being about religious Man. In the second place Barth puts forward an anthropological constructive argument, which reveals his pessimistic anthropology: "Gott und der Mensch, der ich bin, das geht *nicht* zusammen."[9] Barth also argues that human life is characterized by a dualism: "Religion heißt Spaltung des Menschen in zwei Teile ..."[10] Thus, not even religious Man can be depicted in bright hues. In the third place Barth advances the theological constructive argument that his interpretation accords with the reality of religious/human life. No-one is ever capable of fulfilling his or her intentions.[11]

To support his interpretation of ἐγώ as Christian Man living in the two aeons Nygren uses five kinds of arguments: philological, contextual, natural, consistency and constructive. The philological argument is a reference to the change from past to present tense.[12]

The contextual arguments refer to Romans, its content and structure, and thereafter primarily to other epistles in the corpus paulinum. The most important contextual argument from Romans is undoubtedly the reference to the theme and structure of Romans 5–8: "Throughout chapters 5–8 the subject is the meaning of *the Christian life*."[13] Also: "The very same dualism faces us in both chapter 6 and chapter 8. The parallelism in these three chapters can be outlined thus: ..." followed by a table showing these parallels.[14] Reference is also made to other parts of the corpus paulinum e g passages on Paul's view of Man ante and post Christum.[15]

Nygren's natural arguments are of the common sense kind. Of 7:14–25 he says: "... if one comes to the passage without prior assumptions"[16] and "... if the reader, without preconceived view, had let the text speak as it actually is, he would not have construed verses 14–25 as anything else but a character-

---

[7] Barth 1926 p 249, cf p 251: "Religion ist ausbrechender Dualismus."
[8] Barth 1926 p 240. See also p 241.
[9] Barth 1926 p 242.
[10] Barth 1926 p 251.
[11] Barth 1926 p 243: "Sollte je ein ernst zu nehmender Denker, Dichter, Staatsmann oder Künstler in dem, was er getan, wahrhaftig das, was er wollte, wahrhaftig sich selbst wiedergefunden haben?"
[12] Nygren 1944 p 295, 1952 pp 288f.
[13] Nygren 1944 p 294, 1952 p 287.
[14] Nygren 1944 p 302, 1952 pp 295f.
[15] Nygren 1944 pp 292f, 1952 pp 285f and 1944 pp 300f, 1952 p 294.
[16] Nygren 1944 p 291, 1952 p 285.

ization of the present life of the Christian."[17] Thus, Nygren holds that his is the most natural interpretation.

Nygren further puts forward an argument which refers to the aim of rendering the text of Romans as consistent as possible. Arguing against the interpretation of ἐγώ as a person ante Christum, Nygren writes "Since, as we have seen, we encounter so much difficulty and so many exceptions in almost every verse, and since, to make the interpretation fit, it is necessary to take such liberties with what the text says, we have inescapable evidence that the interpretation is *false*."[18]

The constructive argument put forward by Nygren contains the idea of the two aeons which may be understood as both a theological and an anthropological argument. At the end of his discussion of the identity of ἐγώ he states concerning the parallel structure of chs 6–8: "Only if we heed both sides of such facts can we give a true picture of the Christian life; for it is conditioned by the fact that the Christian belongs at the same time to both the new and the old aeons."[19] It is thus clear that it is necessary to grasp the idea of the two aeons in order to arrive at a correct interpretation of the identity of ἐγώ, according to Nygren.

Cranfield interprets ἐγώ as a mature Christian living in this world. His interpretation is made by reference to philological, contextual, natural, consistency and constructive arguments.

Cranfield holds that the introduction of the present tense in 7:14 supports the interpretation that Paul is depicting the situation of the Christian. The contrast with the preceding passage is too marked to be explained away as stylistic decoration. The switch into the present tense indicates that Paul is describing his present situation as a mature Christian.[20]

There are furthermore contextual arguments, which are immediate and refer to the corpus paulinum as well as referring to the structure of Romans.[21] The most important contextual argument referring to the content focuses on how Paul generally describes life ante/post Christum.[22]

Cranfield's natural arguments draw on the history of the interpretation of Romans. However, he acknowledges that authoritative support can also be found for the opposite view.[23] One authority who plays a part in Cranfield's interpretation is Calvin. In commenting on 7:14 Cranfield writes "The only

---

[17] Nygren 1944 p 295, 1952 p 289.
[18] Nygren 1944 p 298, 1952 p 291.
[19] Nygren 1944 p 302, 1952 p 296.
[20] Cranfield 1985 (1) pp 344f.
[21] Cranfield 1985 (1) pp 345f.
[22] Cranfield 1985 (1) p 346: "Not so does Paul describe the unregenerate man", followed by a comparison between 6:17, 18 and 20, and 8:7. A comparable argument for Paul's description of regenerate man is also given on the same page.
[23] Cranfield 1985 (1) pp 345f.

natural way to understand this ἐγώ . . . εἰμι is surely the way indicated by Calvin's comment on the following verse: . . ."[24]

Cranfield also utilises arguments which refer to the consistency of his interpretation. He finds that the apparent inconsistency of Romans 7 and 8 can be resolved if the latter part of ch 7 is said to relate to the Christian. These chapters should be seen as "two different aspects, two contemporaneous realities, of the Christian life, both of which continue so long as the Christian is in the flesh."[25] Furthermore, ". . . it is possible to do justice to the text of Paul (. . .) only if we resolutely hold chapters 7 and 8 together, in spite of the obvious tension between them, . . ."[26]

Finally, Cranfield also refers to two constructive arguments, one anthropological and the other theological. Closely related to, but not included in, a contextual reference, Cranfield states that "In fact, a struggle as serious as that which is here described, can only take place where the Spirit of God is present and active (cf Gal 5.17)."[27] Cranfield is obviously here referring to Christian anthropology, presumably his own. The second constructive argument is necessary if ἐγώ is to be interpreted as a mature Christian. Cranfield asks whether the inability of interpreters to accept the characterization of a Christian as sold under sin can be "the result of failure on our part to realize the full seriousness of the ethical demands of God's law (or of the gospel)."[28] I interpret this as a theological constructive argument in favour of Cranfield's interpretation. Provided he has correctly described the insight of a mature Christian, Cranfield's interpretation is correct.

According to Wilckens' interpretation of 7:13–25, ἐγώ is a person ante Christum, as viewed by the Christian. This interpretation is based on contextual, historical, intentional and constructive arguments.

The contextual arguments are numerous. Primarily they refer to the immediate context of Romans, both its theme and its structure. Wilckens holds that the theme of Romans 7:13–25 concerns the law and from his structuring of Romans 7, taking v 13 as the beginning of the last section, Wilckens finds an explanation of why Paul seems to speak so positively of Man ante Christum. V 13 is the hermeneutical horizon of vv 14–25 and, according to Wilckens, this implies, by extension, that "Was in Röm 7,14–23 positiv vom Ich ausgesagt wird, gilt zum Ruhm des Gesetzes, nicht zum Ruhm des Ich, von dem als solchem vielmehr die negativen Aussagen gelten."[29] Wilckens also pre-

---

[24] Cranfield 1985 (1) p 356.

[25] Ibid.

[26] Ibid.

[27] Cranfield 1985 (1) p 346. See also p 359 on 7:15: "Here battle is joined in earnest in a way that is not possible before a man is sanctified by the Holy Spirit" and p 360.

[28] Cranfield 1985 (1) p 346. The same idea is expressed in the comment on v 14 p 358. See also pp 359f.

[29] Wilckens 1980 (2) p 94. See also pp 74f.

supposes that ch 7 is understood in contrast to chs 6 and 8. Consequently he holds that 7:13–25 cannot concern the Christian.[30] Contextual references outside Romans are mainly to the corpus paulinum, e g to 2 Cor 4:16, and not in support of Wilckens' view, but are on the whole given as possible counter-arguments, which are rejected.[31]

Wilckens also gives a historical argument for the interpretation of ἐγώ as a person ante Christum. I will clarify this argument in the next section which deals with Wilckens' arguments for his interpretation of how Jesus Christ brought salvation to mankind, since the argument carries even more weight there. Let me simply say here that this historical argument, the "Tun-Ergehen-Zusammenhang" argument, contains a description of the contemporary Jewish understanding of sin at the time of Paul. This regarded sin as something caused by human violation of the law whose consequences were irreversible. No matter how many good deeds a person performs, that which has been done cannot be made undone. Wilckens therefore holds that the distinction drawn in v 15 between what ἐγώ would like to do and what he actually does is essentially pointless. It is the act, not the will, that counts.[32]

Wilckens also cites an intentional argument in favour of his interpretation: "Doch Paulus zielt in VV 14ff darauf, zu durchdenken, was es für die Existenz des Sünders bedeutet, daß einerseits das Gesetz selbst 'gut' ist und seine Forderung, das Gute zu tun, auch dort Geltung und Bestand behält, wo andererseits ich im Tun des Bösen der Sünde völlig verfallen bin."[33] Paul thus intended to write something about the sinner, according to Wilckens.

Finally, Wilckens' interpretation is supported by an anthropological and a theological constructive argument. Wilckens holds Paul to be answering questions put by a Jewish opponent in Romans 7. They are discussing the law. Wilckens' anthropological argument is that only the Christian can understand that the law has not been abrogated, despite the abrogation of the condemnation of the law.[34] The theological constructive argument is given in the "Zusammenfassung", but it is implied by the anthropological argument and also, for example, in the judgment of the relation between chs 6, 7 and 8. Wilckens asserts that forgiveness is intended to make the Christian perform righteous deeds, i e obey the law: "... so sehr zielt alle Vergebung christlicher Sünden darauf, daß ihre Kraft, die Liebe, in meinem *Tun* zur Wirkung kommt."[35]

[30] Wilckens 1980 (2) p 86 n 353 and p 92 including n 379.
[31] See e g Wilckens 1980 (2) p 93.
[32] Wilckens 1980 (2) pp 86f.
[33] Wilckens 1980 (2) p 91.
[34] Wilckens 1980 (2) pp 75 and 77: Only from a Christian point of view "... kann begriffen und verstanden werden, daß die abrogatio accusationis legis nicht eine abrogatio legis ist" and p 96 on 7:25a: "Jene illusionsfreie Realistik (...) öffnet sich allererst dem, der in Christus daraus befreit ist."
[35] Wilckens 1980 (2) p 117 (Zusammenfassung).

Thus, it is not possible to explain the differences between Barth's, Nygren's, Cranfield's and Wilckens' interpretations of the identity of ἐγώ in Romans 7:13/14–25 by reference to their pursuit of different kinds of interpretations. Barth does not pursue constructive, Nygren intentional, Cranfield philological and Wilckens historical interpretations. Rather, all pursue combinations of different kinds of interpretations and none pursues fewer than three different kinds. This analysis does not provide sufficient material to draw any conclusions as to whether these combinations of kinds of arguments might be decisive for the different interpretations. Instead, this analysis gives the impression that the variety of arguments which supports the various interpretations of the identity of ἐγώ in Romans 7:13/14–25 is immense. They differ both in kind and content. In order to get an impression of the variety of kinds of arguments used and the way they differ in content the results of this analysis may be illustrated by means of a table. It should be noted that the table shows only the variety of arguments. Indicating the incidence of a kind of argument with a small letter and the differing contents of the arguments with a, b, c and d we get the following result:

Kind	Barth	Nygren	Cranfield	Wilckens
Philological	(a)	b	b	(a)
Contextual	a	b	b	c
Historical				a
Intentional				a
Natural	a	b	a	
Consistency		a	a	
Constructive/anthr	a	b	c	d
Constructive/theol	a	b	c	d

First, we can conclude that historical arguments are only used by Wilckens in support of the interpretation that ἐγώ is a person ante Christum as seen by the Christian. Furthermore, only Nygren and Cranfield refer to consistency arguments for the interpretation of ἐγώ as a Christian. However, all the other different kinds of arguments are advanced in favour both of ἐγώ as a person ante Christum and as a Christian.

Secondly, we can conclude that some kinds of arguments, although used by all these commentators, differ in content. In the case of the philological argument which refers to the change of tense in 7:14, Barth and Wilckens hold it to be a stylistic detail enlivening the text, while Nygren and Cranfield take it to mark a change of subject.[36] The contextual arguments also differ. Wilckens

[36] Barth 1926 p 240 and Wilckens 1980 (2) pp 74f. The philological arguments of Barth and Wilckens were not referred to above, since they are of no major importance for their interpretations, although relevant for this comparison.

keeps to the immediate context, while Barth refers to passages from the whole of the Bible. Nygren and Cranfield share a position in the middle. A peculiarity of the contextual argument referring to chs 6 and 8 is that it supports both basic views, the view that ἐγώ is ante Christum Man and the view that ἐγώ is Christian Man.

Thirdly, Barth, Nygren, Cranfield and Wilckens all use constructive arguments. The majority of the arguments used by Nygren and Cranfield agree basically in content except for the natural arguments. However, Barth and Wilckens, although sharing the same interpretation of the identity of ἐγώ, do not show that correspondence. As far as the constructive arguments are concerned, the interpreters' references all differ in content. They refer, for example, to different anthropologies. Barth's anthropology is deeply pessimistic, and Nygren's dualistic, reflecting the idea of the two aeons, while Cranfield's and Wilckens' are more optimistic concerning the Christian, although not identical, since they draw different conclusions and interpret the identity of ἐγώ differently.

2. Some theological themes

The three problems analysed in this section are taken from the analysis in chapter two and each represents a problem of interpretation from one of the three articles of faith:

1. How does the new covenant relate to the old?
2. How did Jesus Christ bring salvation to human beings?
3. What characterizes Christian life?

There are basically two different answers to the question of how the new covenant relates to the old: the new covenant is in opposition to the old or the new covenant is a continuation of the old, since a fundamental unity exists between the two. Barth and Nygren prefer the first interpretation and Cranfield and Wilckens the second when interpreting Romans. Their different answers can be expressed thus:[37]

Barth: The new covenant is the synthesis of the old covenant, which is abolished, and its opposite.

Nygren: The new covenant is the opposite of the old covenant, although the old points to the new.

Cranfield: The new covenant pursues the same purposes of faith and obedience as the old, the old covenant having created the necessary

---

[37] The formulation of the authors' different answers is intended not just to give a correct description of their interpretations, but also to bring out some characteristics of each of the interpretations. This applies also to the interpretations of the other issues.

conditions for the emergence of the new.

Wilckens: The new covenant is the necessary continuation of the old, making good its failure by pursuing the same purpose of righteousness, although in a new way, through faith and not through works.[38]

The commentaries differ from each other in three important respects concerning this relationship. First, Cranfield and Wilckens support their interpretations by historical arguments, which Barth and Nygren do not. Wilckens argues from a view of Jewish thought as different from the Greek way of thinking. The first allows for contradictions, which are meaningless, according to Greek philosophy. According to Wilckens, Paul has discovered the logic of the Christ event, a dialectical pattern which is more in accordance with Jewish thinking.[39] Cranfield supports his recurrent philological distinction between law and legalism[40] with the historical argument that Paul did not distinguish between the law and legalism, since the distinction was unknown at the time. Had it been known, he would have used "legalism" instead of "the law" and it would thereby have been absolutely clear that Paul did not see the new covenant in opposition to the old.[41]

Secondly, the authors differ concerning the identity of the old covenant, i e they give different constructive arguments. It is possible to have either a narrower or a wider understanding of who is included in the old covenant. Barth and Nygren have a wider, and Cranfield and Wilckens a narrower understanding of the old covenant. Barth includes all mankind, Nygren all but Christians, and Cranfield and Wilckens identify the old covenant primarily with God's covenant with Israel.[42]

These constructive interpretations are in their turn supported by other arguments. Barth and Nygren give primarily constructive arguments for their interpretations, while Cranfield and Wilckens give primarily contextual arguments. Wilckens also gives a historical argument in addition. Barth refers to the theological constructive argument of his view of religion.[43] Nygren refers to the ontological and theological idea of the universal forces of destruction,

---

[38] Cf chapter two: 1. The old covenant, the character of God and the need for salvation.

[39] Wilckens 1978 (1) pp 330f (Zusammenfassung): "Denn Paulus hat hier nichts weniger als die Logik des Christusgeschehens als Logik des Handelns Gottes entdeckt: eine Logik, die denkgeschichtlich völlig neu war." See further pp 330–334, where the difference between Jewish and Greek thought is also developed. Although given in the Zusammenfassung, this is clearly an argument for Wilckens' interpretation of the relation between the covenants.

[40] See e g Cranfield 1985 (1) p 170.

[41] Cranfield 1986 (2) p 853 (essays).

[42] Here Barth's, Nygren's, Cranfield's and Wilckens' interpretations of the law-concept are central, cf chapter one: 2. The law, and chapter two: 1. The old covenant, the character of God and the need for salvation.

[43] Barth 1926 pp 162–164.

the law, which characterizes the old covenant, being one of them.[44] Cranfield supports his interpretation of the old covenant as God's covenant with Israel by a discussion of Paul's attitude to the law in an excursus. Cranfield puts forward Paul's high estimation of the Old Testament law as being God's law. Cranfield's view of Paul's understanding of the old covenant is supported by contextual references primarily to Romans, but also to other parts of the corpus paulinum.[45] Wilckens refers to the historical situation of the Roman congregation. One problem caused by the interpretation of the epistle's emphasis on the Jews is that it is difficult to understand why Paul wrote about the Jews, when addressing himself to a Gentile congregation. According to Wilckens, this is explained by the congregation's close links with the synagogue, of which I have given an account in chapter three.[46] Wilckens' contextual arguments refer primarily to the theme of the epistle.[47]

Thirdly, there are differences which can be explained as differences concerning other constructive arguments. As shown above, Wilckens refers to Paul's use of dialectical thinking. I classified this argument as a historical argument. However, it also has philosophical aspects. Wilckens claims that Paul should be understood using dialectical philosophy, which allows for conflicts (old – new covenant) and yet allows the possibility of syntheses.[48] Wilckens firmly declares that Hegel is one of the few people who has been able to develop a philosophy which corresponds to Paul's thinking.[49] From this Wilckens draws the conclusion that Paul expresses a basic unity between the covenants. However, Barth also draws on dialectical philosophy, but reaches the opposite conclusion.[50] One difference is that Barth also refers to a

---

[44] Nygren 1944 p 223, 1952 p 217: "And the law is not only the total of God's will; it is an objective power which places man under the judgment of condemnation." See also 1944 p 288, 1952 pp 281f.

[45] Cranfield 1986 (2) pp 845f, especially p 846: "So 'the legislation' is reckoned by Paul among the great and glorious privileges of Israel (9.4)."

[46] Wilckens 1978 (1) pp 33–35.

[47] Wilckens 1978 (1) pp 41f: "Paulus entfaltet hier vielmehr das Evangelium der Gottesgerechtigkeit in seiner gleichen Heilskraft für Juden wie Heiden in Dialog mit der *Synagoge*." Cf 1982 (3) p 80 and 1978 (1) p 158

[48] Wilckens 1978 (1) pp 330–334 (Zusammenfassung).

[49] Wilckens 1978 (1) p 334 (Zusammenfassung): "Ja, Hegel hat die Methode seiner ganzen Philosophie durch den ursprünglich paulinischen Gedanken der Versöhnung als Aufhebung der Negation grundgelegt . . .", p 335 (Zusammenfassung) and p 329: "Das 'Mehr' der Gnade besteht darin, daß sie das 'Mehr' der Sünde aufhebt. Da es aber das Gesetz ist, durch das die Sünde zu ihrem 'Mehr' gekommen ist, hat es dadurch die Voraussetzung für den Herrschaftsantritt der Gnade in Kraft gesetzt. Insofern hat es in seiner radikal negativen Funktion auf der Adam-Seite zugleich eine mittelbar soteriologische Bedeutung." This shows that Wilckens really uses the dialectical pattern and not refers to it only in the Zusammenfassungen.

[50] See e g Barth 1926 p 155, where an explicit reference to dialectics is made concerning the relation between Adam and Christ and Barth clarifies: "Also: daß die unanschauliche Pragmatik der neuen Welt zwar in ihrer Form dieselbe ist wie die der alten, in ihrer Bedeutung und Kraft aber nicht dieselbe, sondern die schlechthin überlegene, die gerade umgekehrte, das ist nun noch zu überlegen und auszusprechen."

dualistic ontology, i e he also gives an ontological constructive argument. The dialectic concerns not just guilt and grace, but the insuperable gulf which stretches between God's world and ours: "In der radikalen Aufhebung der geschichtlichen und seelichen Wirklichkeit, in der umfassenden Relativierung ihrer Stufen und Gegensätze erscheint ihre wahre, ihre ewige Bedeutung."[51] Another aspect of the difference discernible here concerning the philosophical arguments is that Barth stresses the dualism, while Wilckens stresses the synthesis of the dialectical scheme.

Important for Nygren's interpretation of the relation between the covenants is the constructive argument of the two aeons. Nygren does not share the dialectical philosophical position, but he does basically share Barth's radical dualism, primarily expressed in this idea, for which Nygren finds support in the context. The idea of the two aeons is very complex and can be understood in at least three ways. (1) It is a basic theological idea, a way of expressing God's work of salvation. This is how I generally interpret it. (2) It is an ontological idea, which aims at describing the state of things. However, it is not identical with Barth's dualistic ontology, since the two aeons are both real to Christians here and now. (3) It is an anthropological idea, since it expresses the ambiguity of Christian life.[52] (1) and (2) are the most important here.[53]

Cranfield supports his interpretation with a theological and an anthropological constructive argument, which describe the character of God and the relation between God and human beings is their moral accountability: their relation is thus basically moral. This is expressed in God's covenant with Israel, which sets the necessary forensic background for the new to appear. "If sin, which was already present and disastrously active in mankind, though as yet nowhere clearly visible and defined, were ever to be decisively defeated and sinners forgiven in a way worthy of the goodness and mercy of God and recreated in newness of life, it was first of all necessary that sin should increase somewhere among men in the sense of becoming clearly manifest."[54]

---

[51] Barth 1926 p 52, cf p 142: "Und es ist das Nicht-Sein der ersten Welt, das das Sein der zweiten ist, gerade wie die zweite ihren Seinsgrund nur im Nicht-Sein der ersten hat."

[52] Nygren 1944 pp 28–33, 1952 pp 20–26. (1) the theological sense, 1944 p 30, 1952 pp 22f: "Against this background the meaning of the gospel is seen most clearly. To us who are in bondage to the dominion of the age of death comes the gospel with its message that the new age, the age of life, has burst upon us." (2) the ontological sense, 1944 p 31, 1952 pp 23f on the terminology of aeons: "But Paul's word helps to make clear that he speaks of two different orders of existence". (3) the anthropological sense, closely related to the ontological sense, 1944 p 33, 1952 p 26: "Basic to this view of Paul's are two facts: one, that in this world we belong to death's domain; the other, that through Christ, God has burst in upon this world with the dominion of life".

[53] Nygren 1944 pp 79f (theological sense) and 85f (ontological sense), 1952 pp 71f and 77f. On the unity between the two aeons see 1944 pp 174f, 1952 pp 166f.

[54] Cranfield 1985 (1) pp 292f. See also 1986 (2) pp 850f (essays).

The covenants are viewed as two stages in the development of the moral relation between God and Man.

Thus, the different interpretations of the relation between the new and the old covenants as being opposed to (Barth and Nygren) or in accord with (Cranfield and Wilckens) each other are supported by constructive arguments by all the authors. A similar philosophical argument was used by Barth and Wilckens for the two different interpretations. On this issue, Barth's and Nygren's interpretations differ from Cranfield's and Wilckens' in that Cranfield and Wilckens combine their constructive arguments with historical and contextual arguments, and Barth and Nygren do not. Barth's and Nygren's interpretations of the relation between the two covenants are primarily constructive.

Let us turn to the second problem of interpretation which concerns how Jesus Christ brought salvation to human beings. In chapter two we concluded that Barth's, Nygren's, Cranfield's and Wilckens' interpretations of Paul's view of atonement pointed to different doctrines of atonement. The doctrines indicated were in Barth's commentary a dialectic, in Nygren's a dramatic, in Cranfield's a penal and in Wilckens' commentary a satisfaction doctrine of atonement within a cultic context. One of the key questions answered by such a doctrine is: how did Jesus Christ bring salvation to human beings? The commentators' different interpretations of Paul's view of atonement may be clarified by stating the answers they give to this question in their commentaries:

Barth: God's work in Jesus Christ was necessary to bring forth the new human being, who lives in God.

Nygren: In Jesus Christ God overcame the four forces of destruction.

Cranfield: Jesus Christ became the object of God's wrath and human beings were delivered at God's own expense.

Wilckens: Jesus Christ is God's cultic sacrifice by which the consequences of human sin are abolished.[55]

What arguments are given for these interpretations? First, we can see that, as far as the identity of ἐγώ is concerned, the same philological argument is used again for different interpretations. According to Nygren, God's sending forth of Christ as ἱλαστήριον (3:25) refers primarily to the revelatory aspect of God's act in Christ; according to Cranfield, it indicates that it was connected with the wrath of God; while according to Wilckens, it indicates the cultic context.[56]

---

[55] Cf chapter two: 2. Atonement and righteousness.
[56] Nygren 1944 pp 166f, 1952 pp 158f. Cranfield 1985 (1) pp 216f and Wilckens 1978 (1) pp 190–193.

Secondly, Wilckens argues primarily with references to modern exegesis, i e a natural argument, and a historical argument. He asserts that modern historical exegesis at least puts in question the Anselmian interpretation of the doctrine of atonement and many also support a new understanding of sin and unrighteousness, expressed by his term "Tun-Ergehen-Zusammenhang", which freely translates as: connections between deeds and their consequences. According to him, Jewish tradition and Paul both focus on the active aspect of unrighteousness. An unrighteous person performs unrighteous deeds. These unrighteous deeds result in guilt or debt, which is thought of as a kind of reality. New good deeds cannot take away the consequences of unrighteous deeds. However, the Jewish cult provided the means for the Jews to influence these consequences. This is the background to Paul's view of atonement, supported by the context of Romans, which denies Anselm's satisfaction theory, since it does not grasp the meaning of sacrifice. I have understood this to mean that the sacrifice can change the "Tun-Ergehen-Zusammenhang" ontologically and thus does not change the wrath of God forensically.[57]

Thirdly, the same constructive arguments put forward by Barth, Nygren and Cranfield concerning the relation between the covenants are held to support their interpretations of the way in which Jesus Christ brought salvation to human beings. Barth refers to the dialectical pattern and the dualistic ontology, Nygren to the idea of the two aeons in its theological sense and Cranfield to the moral relation between God and Man.[58]

Thus, Barth's, Nygren's, Cranfield's and Wilckens' different interpretations of the way in which Jesus Christ brought salvation to mankind can be

---

[57] This historical argument (and its natural correlative) is most clearly expressed in the excursus "Zum Verständnis der Sühne-Vorstellung", Wilckens 1978 (1) pp 233–243, but occurs frequently also in the "Erklärung" sections, see e g pp 195f. For the references to modern exegesis, see pp 234f. On the basis of this, Wilckens also rejects later forms of doctrines of atonement, pp 241–243 and 201 (Zusammenfassung).

[58] Barth 1926 p 174, where the resurrection is characterized as "Möglichwerden des dem Menschen Unmöglichen" and p 180: "Gnade ist die *göttliche* Möglichkeit des Menschen, die ihn als solche seiner eigenen Möglichkeit beraubt." See also pp 260f on the ontological idea, where Barth writes that God did not send his son "um hier irgend etwas zu verändern", but to establish "die neue Schöpfung, in der Schöpfer und Geschöpf nicht zwei, sondern eins sind."
Nygren 1944 p 167, 1952 p 159: "The old aeon was the time of God's wrath. (. . .) So in the age that has now come, in the new aeon which has burst upon us through Christ, God reveals His righteousness, . . ."
Cranfield 1985 (1) pp 267f: ". . . Christ's death was the means by which God pardoned us without in any way condoning our sin and so laid aside His hostility towards us in a way that was worthy of His goodness and love and consistent with His constant purpose of mercy for us, and, on the other hand, it was the means by which He demonstrated His love for us and so broke our hostility toward Himself." See also p 217.

explained by their different combinations of arguments. The kinds of arguments combined not only determine the interpretation, but the combination in itself shapes the arguments. Nygren, Cranfield and Wilckens interpret Paul's answer to the question of how Jesus Christ brought salvation to human beings differently, but they refer to the same philological argument in the sense that they all refer to the meaning of ἱλαστήριον in 3:25. However, there are clear connections between their interpretations of ἱλαστήριον in the philological arguments and the contents of their historical and constructive arguments. Nygren points to the revelatory aspect of ἱλαστήριον, which corresponds to his constructive assumption of the two aeons, of which the second has been revealed by God. Cranfield stresses the connection with the wrath of God, which corresponds to his constructive assumption of the moral relation between God and Man. Finally, Wilckens refers to the cultic meaning of ἱλαστήριον, corresponding to his account of the "Tun-Ergehen-Zusammenhang". Barth's interpretation, however, does not fit into this pattern. He argues primarily with reference to constructive arguments.

The third part of this analysis of the theological themes concerns the question of what characterizes Christian life. None of these commentators would deny that justification has consequences for the morals of the Christian, according to Romans. However, they differ concerning the importance of this. Some hold Christian life to be characterized primarily by obedience, whereas others believe the prime characteristic of Christian life is something else, e g a new status or perspective. I call the first view the transformation view and the second the simul view. The allusion of the latter to Luther is deliberate and the reader may well associate Calvin with the former. Barth and Nygren hold the simul view to be in accordance with a correct interpretation of Romans, while Cranfield and Wilckens understand the transformation view to be in accordance with a correct interpretation of Romans:

Barth: Christian life is characterized by the tension between this world and God's.
Nygren: Christian life is characterized by the tension between the two aeons.
Cranfield: Christian life is characterized by obedience.
Wilckens: Christian life is characterized by obedience.[59]

The contextual arguments concerning the character of Christian life are important to Nygren, Cranfield and Wilckens. Again the context supports both views. A difference can be discerned in that Cranfield and Wilckens refer to

---

[59] Cf chapter two: 3. Christian life and eschatology.

the connection between chs 5–8, for example, in the main part of the epistle and the parenesis passage from ch 12. The main contextual argument for the simul view relates to chs 5–8.[60]

Luther plays an important role as far as the natural arguments put forward by Nygren are concerned, while Cranfield refers to Calvin.[61] Barth, although agreeing with Luther on the simul view, strongly objects to his view that Christian ethics are not based on grace.[62] Wilckens does not draw heavily on these authorities either. Wilckens' prime reconstructive argument is the historical argument of the "Tun-Ergehen-Zusammenhang". Just as sin necessarily brings forth unrighteousness, which leads to death, so forgiveness brings forth righteousness, which leads to life, in Wilckens' interpretation of Romans. "Wie die Sünde ihre Wirklichkeit im konkreten Tun hat, so auch die Gerechtigkeit".[63]

Several by now familiar constructive arguments recur. Barth refers to ontological dualism, Nygren to the theological idea of the two aeons and in Cranfield, the moral relation between God and Man is presupposed (theological and anthropological arguments).[64]

However, some other constructive arguments also occur. They refer in the first place to different anthropologies. Barth and Nygren hold that Christian life is in a sense ambiguous. According to them, this ambiguity is caused by the fact that the Christian already belongs to God and yet continues to exist in

---

[60] Nygren 1944 p 302, 1952 p 295, where chs 6–8 are all said to contain the simul aspect and 1944 p 269, 1952 p 262. Cranfield 1986 (2) p 592: "The first eleven chapters of Romans have already made it clear that the life, which, according to 1.17, is the destiny of the man who is righteous by faith, is a life of obedience to God." In 12:1–15:13 the exhortation follows, p 594. Wilckens 1982 (3) p 2 on 12:1–2: "... es geht im folgenden um die Konkretisierung dessen, was Paulus grundsätzlich über den christlichen Wandel in Röm 6–8 gesagt hat, im Blick auf das christliche Zusammenleben in der Gemeinde."

[61] Nygren 1944 p 328, 1952 p 322, where Luther is quoted without mentioning his name: "The Christian is *simul justus et peccator*, both righteous and sinner at the same time." Cranfield 1985 (1) p 295 including n 1, where Cranfield refers to Calvin in support of his view that Paul is concerned "to insist that justification has inescapable moral implications" in ch 6 and holding the opposite view "is a profane absurdity". See also p 594 n 1.

[62] Barth 1926 p 416.

[63] Wilckens 1980 (2) p 40 (Zusammenfassung). Cf pp 17–19 on the Old Testament background of the "Tun-Ergehen-Zusammenhang" and its application to ch 6. See also Wilckens 1978 (1) pp 295–298.

[64] Barth 1926 pp 296f: "Diesseits der Auferstehung aber ist Religion das letzte Wort (...) Daher die Beunruhigung und Sehnsucht ..." and pp 449f. Nygren 1944 p 270, 1952 p 263, where the theological meaning of the idea is expressed as God's victory over the destructive powers. Cranfield 1986 (2) pp 593 and 861f (essays).

this world.[65] Cranfield and Wilckens on the other hand understand Paul to mean that the Spirit changes the conditions of life or character of the Christian and makes him obedient, although not denying the difficulties caused by the unfulfilled nature of Christian faith. Cranfield understands this simply in terms of the Spirit enabling the Christian to obey God. Wilckens holds that the mind of the Christian is renewed through baptism.[66]

Secondly they all refer to arguments which are particular to themselves. Barth uses the theological argument of the double predestination to support his interpretation of the simul view of Christian life. According to Barth, human life is ambiguous, because God has predestined everyone both to damnation and salvation. Thus, as sin and grace are dialectical opposites, which the Christian experiences as damnation and salvation, Christian ethical life points to the human plight and human opportunity. Barth can therefore say "Das Problem der 'Ethik' ist identisch mit dem der 'Dogmatik' ..."[67] Cranfield supports his transformation view of Christian life by arguments which point in the direction of a theological constructive argument which holds obedience to be a prerequisite for the attainment of ultimate salvation.[68] One theological constructive argument referred to by Wilckens has already been touched upon. Wilckens holds that Romans puts forward a factual view of baptism, that is, baptism is not merely a symbolic act – something actually happens. The Christian receives the Spirit and is granted both the knowledge and assurance of God's love and the ability to render love effective.[69]

Thus, first, the different interpretations of the character of Christian life can be explained by reference to the use of different contextual arguments. Barth and Nygren refer to a closer context for their interpretations of the ambi-

---

[65] Barth 1926 p 296: "Also unanschaulich herkommend vom Geiste Gottes geht der Mensch anschaulich ganz und gar hinein in eine unendliche Zweideutigkeit" and p 446: "Denn was immer von positiven *oder* negativen Möglichkeiten genannt werden mag, sind Möglichkeiten des *Menschen*, es sind zweideutige Möglichkeiten ..." Nygren 1944 p 425, 1952 p 426: "Again and again, in the preceding parts of the letter, we have been reminded of the tension in the life of the Christian due to the fact that it must be lived *in this aeon*" and 1944 pp 306f, 1952 pp 299f. It should be noticed that Nygren still has good hopes concerning the possibilities of Christian transformation in this world: "His mind and conduct must not bear the mark of this age; a genuine *metamorphosis of mind and conduct* must take place." Nygren 1944 p 418, 1952 p 418.

[66] Cranfield 1986 (2) pp 593f: "In chapter 8 the necessity of obedience is set forth in terms of the gift of the Spirit. To be in Christ is to be indwelt by His Spirit, and the Spirit of Christ is the Holy Spirit, who establishes God's law in its true character and function as 'unto life' (7.10) and 'spiritual' (7.14) ..." Cf p 861 (essays). Wilckens 1982 (3) p 7: "Die Vernunft des Christen wird durch diese Erneuerung fähig, in jeder konkreten Situation wahrzunehmen, zu beurteilen und zu entscheiden (δοκμάζειν), was Gottes Wille ist ..." See also 1980 (2) pp 20–22 and 129.

[67] Barth 1926 p 417.

[68] Cranfield 1985 (1) p 433, where Cranfield assumes that sanctification is "an intermediate link between justification and glorification".

[69] Wilckens 1980 (2) p 15: "Die Taufe bezeugt nicht, sondern bewirkt die Teilhabe an Christi Tod", pp 24 (Zusammenfassung) and 129–131.

guity of Christian life and Cranfield and Wilckens to a wider context for their interpretation that Christian life is characterized by obedience. However, this difference cannot be generalized in respect of these commentaries, cf above on the contextual arguments for the interpretations of ἐγώ, where Barth refers to the widest and Wilckens to the most immediate context.

Secondly, we can observe that the Reformers continue to exert an influence over biblical exegesis in the twentieth century. This accounts not only for Nygren's and Cranfield's commentaries, but also for Barth's and Wilckens'. However, it is more usual for Barth and Wilckens to refer to them en passant or by way of illustration than as actual support for their interpretations.[70]

Thirdly, we can conclude that several arguments recur and thus constitute a kind of interpretive basis for the commentators. We recognize the anthropological arguments from the interpretation of the identity of ἐγώ, Barth's ontological dualism, Nygren's idea of the two aeons, and Cranfield's moral relation, all of which are constructive arguments. Wilckens' historical reference to the "Tun-Ergehen-Zusammenhang" also keeps coming back.

In conclusion to this analysis of the interpretations of some theological themes in Romans we might ask: how then can the different interpretations of these themes given by Barth, Nygren, Cranfield and Wilckens be explained in terms of different kinds of interpretations? Two things can be stated as results of this analysis. First, these interpreters all refer to combinations of kinds of interpretations. Different philological, contextual and historical arguments are combined with different constructive arguments. These combinations are interdependent in content.[71] Secondly, each commentary has an interpretive basis, which keeps guiding the authors' interpretations. In Barth's, Nygren's and Cranfield's commentaries this basis consists of constructive assumptions like Barth's dualistic ontology, Nygren's concept of the two aeons and Cranfield's moral relation between God and Man. In Wilckens' commentary the interpretive basis is historical, referring to the historical situation of Paul and the Romans or to ideas current at the time. Wilckens however also relies on constructive arguments, but these vary too much in content to constitute an interpretive basis.

---

[70] Barth 1926 pp 526–528 and Wilckens 1980 (2) p 85 n 344 and 1982 (3) pp 36f n 173. However, the discussion with the Reformers is on the whole localised in the excursuses, as 1980 (2) pp 107–110 and 1982 (3) pp 49–55. Cf Nygren 1944 pp 24f, 1952 pp 17f and Cranfield 1986 (2) Index IV.

[71] Cf the table above on p 80.

3. Some general remarks

The commentaries' general remarks on Romans are not interpretations in the strict sense. The same kinds of arguments are nevertheless put forward by Barth, Nygren, Cranfield and Wilckens to support their various general remarks and their interpretations of ἐγώ and some of the theological themes. In this section the different kinds of arguments are thus not criteria of kinds of interpretation. This analysis does not aim to examine whether the differences relating to the general remarks can be explained by the authors' pursuit of different kinds of interpretations. The purpose of this analysis is to examine whether these differences can be explained by the authors' use of different kinds of arguments and by the contents of those arguments.

As in the earlier sections of this chapter, I have limited the number of questions I want to discuss. One question from each section in chapter three is analysed, namely:

1. What is the significance of Paul's Jewish origin?
2. What is the basic difficulty about the weak and the strong in 14:1–15:13?
3. What was Paul's purpose in writing Romans?
4. What is the key to the interpretation of the theme of justification through faith?

These four questions have been selected from chapter three for the following reasons: question one throws light on a problem about which there has been debate both in Sweden and abroad.[72] Question two was chosen from the questions posed in the second section because the other questions raised there are dealt with elsewhere. The commentators' differing attitudes to historical knowledge are dealt with in chapter five in connection with their differences of purpose, and the identity of the Jews and the Gentiles comes close to the issue of the relation between the two covenants above. The arguments advanced for Paul's purpose are especially interesting in relation to the discussion of the commentators' purposes in chapter five, and the analysis also brings out a kind of argument which is not very frequently used. Question four, finally, sums up the fourth section in chapter three.

The first general remark to be analysed in this chapter concerns the significance of Paul's Jewish origins. Paul's Jewish origin is used in basically two ways for the interpretation of Romans. It is taken to be important for Paul's understanding of what Christianity is not; or it is taken to be important for his understanding of what Christianity is. Barth and Nygren share the first view and Cranfield and Wilckens the second. The different answers given by the four authors are:

---

[72] See e g Stendahl 1976 and Sanders 1977 and 1983. For the Swedish debate see Unger 1980.

Barth: Paul's Jewish origin is important for the proper understanding of his view of what Christianity is not.

Nygren: Paul's Jewish origin is important for the proper understanding of his view of what Christianity is not.

Cranfield: Paul's Jewish origin is important for the proper understanding of his view of Christianity.

Wilckens: Paul's Jewish origin constitutes the background for the proper understanding of his view of Christianity.[73]

Although contextual and historical arguments exist, for example, which support these views of Paul's Jewish origin, I would like to draw attention only to one theological constructive argument. It is obvious that Barth, Nygren, Cranfield and Wilckens hold different views concerning the uniqueness of Christianity in relation to Judaism. Barth's negative view of religion makes him critical of Paul's Jewish period. However, this should not be understood in too unsophisticated terms. Barth holds that religion is the highest opportunity open to mankind, although it is impossible in the same way that it is impossible to draw a bird in flight. That is to say that although religion always falls short of the goal (human beings can never achieve a relationship with God by their own endeavours), it remains the highest human endeavour.[74] Nygren hints at his view of comparative religion. According to Nygren, the goal of all religions other than Christianity is the establishment of human righteousness. Paul's life as a Jew must therefore be the opposite of his Christian life, which is characterized by the righteousness from God.[75] Cranfield and Wilckens reject this negative view of Judaism, although they do not use it as an argument here. Rather, a more positive view of Judaism is presupposed right through their commentaries, as we have seen for example in the analysis of the relation between the two covenants which implies a different understanding of the unique nature of Christianity.

As Wilckens points out, the higher estimation of Judaism is a post-war feature.[76] The horrors of the holocaust have changed the presuppositions for the interpretation of Romans. Many scholars have contributed to this change, among them Ed P Sanders and Krister Stendahl.[77] This difference can thus be explained historically. But this goes beyond the purpose of the present study. In terms of different kinds of arguments, the various remarks of the interpreters on Paul's Jewish origins can be explained by their different understandings of the uniqueness of Christianity in relation to Judaism, i e to their

---

[73] Cf chapter three: 1. The apostle Paul.

[74] Barth 1926 p 4, where Paul's gospel is characterized as "keine religiöse Botschaft" and p 129, where Barth writes that Saul is "aufgehoben worden". See also pp 161–163.

[75] Nygren 1944 pp 21f, 1952 pp 14f.

[76] Wilckens 1980 (2) pp 267f (Zusammenfassung).

[77] Sanders 1977 and 1983 and Stendahl 1976.

different theological constructive arguments.

The second general remark which will be analysed in this chapter concerns the fundamental problem of the weak and the strong in 14:1–15:13. It is possible to hold either that the fundamental problem concerns both groups and articulate the content of the problem thereafter, or to hold that the fundamental problem relates primarily to a misunderstanding of the weak, whereupon the fundamental problem becomes the problem per se, which threatens the unity of the congregation. Barth and Cranfield take the first view and Nygren and Wilckens the second:

Barth: Fundamentally, the problem concerns the human dilemma.
Nygren: Fundamentally, the problem concerns the unity of the congregation.
Cranfield: Fundamentally, the problem concerns Christian freedom versus the spiritual development of the weak.
Wilckens: Fundamentally, the problem concerns the unity of the church.[78]

Before going further I should point out that none of these authors denies that the strong are, in a sense, right. The difference between Barth and Cranfield on the one hand, and Nygren and Wilckens on the other, is that Barth and Cranfield give more emphasis to the problematic aspects of the attitude of the strong.[79]

The decisive point of difference concerning the view of the fundamental problem of Romans 14:1–15:13 is the authors' different understandings of the content of the gospel, i e the different theological constructive arguments they employ. These arguments are connected with other arguments specific to each interpreter. In Barth's commentary the view of the gospel is connected with contextual arguments, in Cranfield's with a philological argument, in Nygren's with another constructive argument and in Wilckens' with a historical argument.

Barth and Cranfield hold the essence of the gospel to correspond to the problem discussed. According to Barth, Paul understands the gospel to be opposed to all that is human. This is what both the strong and the weak forget. The fundamental problem is that they pay too much attention to what is human.[80] According to Cranfield, the gospel is not compatible in all respects

---

[78] Cf chapter three: 2. The Romans and Paul's opponents.

[79] For their interpretations of the strong as being in a sense right see Barth 1926 p 498 and Cranfield 1986 (2) p 713.

[80] Barth 1926 p 489 where Barth addresses himself to the reader and says: "Greift die 'grosse Störung' nicht *durch*, wird sie nicht zur Krisis *jeder* Bewußtheit (auch und gerade derjenigen, die sie selbst zum Inhalt hat!), bleibt nicht Gott allein übrig, (. . .) so war Alles miteinander ein tönendes Erz und eine klingende Schelle." I e both opinions are in a sense wrong, since they are human, cf pp 466f.

with human freedom; instead it corresponds in Romans to obedience. Both the strong and the weak are disobedient.[81]

In Barth's commentary the understanding of the essence of the problem is also supported by contextual arguments which refer to the theme and structure of Romans. Barth holds that Romans ends with an exhortation to a free experiment in living, "*freie* Lebensversuch", which is free in the sense that it is free of all that pertains to this world.[82] He furthermore understands Paul to express the abolitionary aspect of this freedom (freedom is in opposition to all that is human) by denying everything he has written so far at the end of the epistle. "Denn wenn der Römerbrief zum Schluß sich selbst aufhebt, indem er ausgerechnet gerade den Verständigen, den Empfänglichen, den prädisponierten Paulinern unter seinen Lesern ein ausdrücklichstes Halt! entgegenstellt, so bewährt er gerade *damit* und *nur* damit sich selbst."[83] Several constructive arguments may also be recognized: the dualistic ontology,[84] the pessimistic anthropology[85] and the theological idea of the double predestination, which implies the rejection of all that is human.[86]

Cranfield employs a philological argument concerning the concept of faith to support his understanding of the conflict. He distinguishes between different kinds of faith. The weak lack the faith which permits certain actions, while the strong convey a weakness concerning basic faith, "fides qua creditur", since they assert their own freedom at the expense of the weak.[87] The strong show thereby that they have failed to grasp the essence of the gospel.

Nygren and Wilckens believe that the fundamental problem relates to the unity of the congregation (Nygren) and of the church (Wilckens). This is because they understand the essence of the gospel to be unity. According to Nygren, Paul understands the gospel to concern not this or that way of living, so much as one's own state of being. The Christian belongs to Christ, and weak or strong does not really matter: Christian freedom implies the rights of both

---

[81] Cranfield 1986 (2) p 717: "...it is more probable that Paul is in this verse warning the strong against an even more serious danger, namely, the danger that they may by a selfish insistence on the exercise of their freedom bring reproach upon an ἀγαθόν which is even more precious than their freedom, that ἀγαθόν, which is both theirs (ὑμῶν) and also at the same time the ἀγαθόν of their weak fellow-Christians, the gospel itself, ..." For the strong connection between gospel and obedience see 1985 (1) p 90, where Cranfield identifies faith with obedience.

[82] Barth 1926 p 487.

[83] Barth 1926 p 489.

[84] Barth 1926 p 501: "Unrein vor Gott ist *Alles* und eben darum im Besonderen *nichts*, ..."

[85] Barth 1926 pp 497f.

[86] Barth 1926 p 495: "*Gerade* der Gedanke an die Prädestination, von der der Schwache keine Ahnung hat, wird also den Starken veranlassen, sich mit jenem durchaus in eine Reihe zu stellen."

[87] Cranfield 1986 (2) pp 697f.

weak and strong.[88] Wilckens believes that Paul understands the essence of the gospel to be closely related to the unity both of believers and, in a wider perspective, mankind. Any controversy therefore threatens what it is all about.[89]

Nygren relies on the theological constructive argument of the distinction between law and gospel to support his view of the conflict. According to Nygren, to maintain that either party is right would be to yield to the law. According to the gospel, no-one can be rejected because of his or her behaviour.[90]

Wilckens employs a historical argument to argue for the view that the fundamental conflict concerns the unity of the church. The unity of the Roman congregation was threatened by the God-fearers' struggle for freedom from the law, while other Gentile Christians were more cautious and furthermore took seriously the difficulty that it was impossible to tell whether the meat sold on the markets was ritually clean.[91] Wilckens also refers to a peculiar anthropological argument. He maintains that since all human beings are rational and since they are therefore all capable of a relation to God, no-one has the right to tell anyone else that he is wrong about something he thinks God wants him to do.[92]

Thus Barth's, Nygren's, Cranfield's and Wilckens' understanding of what the conflict between the weak and the strong is really about can be explained by the different ways in which they combine their arguments. Their argumentation has certain affinities with their argumentation for their interpretations of the way in which Jesus Christ brought salvation to human beings. In that context, a common philological argument acquired different meanings in combination with historical and constructive arguments. Here a common constructive argument acquires different meanings in combination with philo-

---

[88] Nygren 1944 p 443, 1952 p 444: "Paul here contends for Christian freedom, for the right of both weak and strong. (. . .) it is only in this way that he can be true to the gospel. But if he had prescribed a Christian course of action, as was desired of him, it would have involved a surrender of the evangelical position" and 1944 p 445, 1952 pp 445f.

[89] Wilckens 1982 (3) pp 106–109. On p 106 Wilckens asserts that Paul sees the conflict in the light of the salvation historical relation between Israel and the Gentiles. The idea is developed in the Zusammenfassung p 109: "Nur so, durch gemeinsame Errettung zusammen mit allen Heiden, hat Gott die eigentliche Wahrheit der Erwählung Israels verwirklicht und sich selbst als der Erwählende verherrlicht." Cf pp 81–86 and 86 (Zusammenfassung), where Wilckens makes it clear that the unity of the congregation is implied in that the church is the body of Christ.

[90] Nygren 1944 pp 443f, 1952 p 444: "If he had declared that all Christians were to follow the example 'of the weak' and abstain from eating meat and drinking wine, the legalistic character of such an enactment would be clear. Or, if he had chosen the other position and decreed that all Christians should, without misgivings, eat meat and drink wine, the result would likewise have been a victory for legalism."

[91] Wilckens 1982 (3) pp 86f (Zusammenfassung), cf 1978 (1) pp 39–41.

[92] Wilckens 1982 (3) pp 98f (Zusammenfassung). The argument is Christologically motivated by the statement that Christ died "für jeden persönlich", p 98.

logical (Cranfield), contextual (Barth), historical (Wilckens) and other constructive arguments (Barth, Nygren and Wilckens). Thus, the different kinds and types of arguments are dependent on each other as concerning the interpretation of salvation through Jesus Christ. It should be noted that while this result may not be surprising where a question of high systematic theological interest such as that touching upon Christology is concerned, this is also true of the more historical question of what the conflict in Romans 14:1–15:13 was really about.

The third general remark to be analysed in this chapter concerns Paul's purpose in writing Romans. The different views of Paul's purpose in Romans relate to the question of whether the content of the epistle was in any way dependent on Paul's circumstances and those of the Romans or not. Barth and Nygren think only the content of the message is decisive, while Cranfield and Wilckens take also the circumstances into account. Their answers may be summarized thus:

Barth: Paul's prime purpose was to expound his theology, and he was motivated by his call.

Nygren: Paul's prime purpose was to expound his theology, and he was motivated by his call.

Cranfield: Paul's prime purpose was to present his theology, and he was motivated by his missionary plans.

Wilckens: Paul's prime purpose was to expound his theology, and he was motivated by the threat to the unity of the church.[93]

A major point of difference concerns the intentional arguments presented in favour of Nygren's, Cranfield's and Wilckens' general remarks about Paul's purpose.

Nygren understands Paul's intention to be that of coming to terms with his past. The contextual reference to chs 9–11 is taken as support for this view.[94] Cranfield and Wilckens think Paul's intentions were directed more towards the current situation and the future. Cranfield thinks Paul wanted simply to introduce himself to the people with whom he hoped to cooperate.[95] Wilckens understands Paul's epistle to the Romans as an important part of Paul's

---

[93] Cf chapter three: 3. The purpose and character of Romans.

[94] Nygren 1944 p 16, 1952 pp 8f: "Instead of an accounting with his opponents, we see Paul's accounting with himself, with his past; for he too had formerly walked the way of salvation by works. To the very fact that he had been hindered from realizing his purpose to visit the Roman congregation, and therefore had to write to it as a congregation that was strange to him, are we indebted for our possession, in this epistle, of Christianity's incomparably remarkable document, where the gospel speaks, more clearly than anywhere else, against the law as a background" and 1944 pp 359–361, 1952 pp 356–358.

[95] Cranfield 1986 (2) pp 817f (essays).

struggle for the unity of the church. His intention was to resolve a conflict in the church.[96]

Barth refers less to Paul's intentions than to an ontological constructive argument. Paul's purpose is independent of the circumstances since Romans is about God and God is divorced from this world. God-talk is always independent of earthly circumstances.[97]

One similarity and one more difference should be pointed out. First, Nygren, Cranfield and Wilckens give contextual arguments in favour of their opinions. They all refer to the unity of the epistle, its structure and train of thought.[98] Again the weakness of the contextual arguments is shown. Secondly, Wilckens refers again to Paul's historical situation. The reason why Paul had to struggle so hard for the unity of the church was that he understood this to be the proper consequence of God's salvation historical plan.[99]

Nygren, Cranfield and Wilckens thus support their different understandings of Paul's purpose in Romans with intentional and contextual arguments. The context again shows that it is capable of supporting two opposing views. However, the constructive and historical arguments of Barth and Wilckens respectively explain their different understandings of Paul's purpose. Since Barth holds God-talk not to be dependent on anything worldly, it is alien to his ontology to seek Paul's purpose in temporal circumstances. Similarly, since Wilckens takes the view that Paul is involved in a political struggle for the unity of the church, he holds that historical circumstances were decisive as far as Paul's intentions in Romans were concerned.

The fourth general remark to be analysed in this chapter is which key to use in order to interpret the justification through faith theme in Romans. I must begin by drawing attention to the imbalance that exists between the authors

---

[96] Wilckens 1978 (1) p 46, where Paul is said to be involved in the conflict between Jews and Christians as well as between Jewish and Gentile Christians. "Beiderorts sind Gefahren für sein bisheriges und künftiges Missionswerk zu befürchten. So gestaltet sich ihm wie von selbst der *Römerbrief* zugleich als Vorbereitung seiner Verteidigungsrede in *Jerusalem*."

[97] Barth 1926 p 4: "Gerade als Apostel ohne ein geordnetes Verhältnis zur menschlichen Gemeinschaft in ihrer geschichtlichen Wirklichkeit, von da aus gesehen vielmehr eine nur als Ausnahme mögliche, ja unmögliche Erscheinung. Das Recht dieser seiner Stellung und die Glaubwürdigkeit seiner Rede ruhen in Gott." See also p 517.

[98] Nygren 1944 p 24, 1952 p 17: "It is because he has this one tremendous fact to proclaim that his presentation shows its unbreakable unity." Cranfield 1986 (2) p 818 (essays): "...once having decided to attempt to compose a summary of the gospel as he had come to understand it, he allowed the inner logic of the gospel as he understood it itself to determine, at any rate for the most part, the structure and contents of what was now going to be the main body of his letter." Wilckens 1978 (1) p 15: "Der Römerbrief unterscheidet sich von allen übrigen Paulusbriefen darin, daß der Apostel am Ende des Briefeingangs (1,14–17) ein Thema markiert, das er im folgenden durch das ganze Briefkorpus hindurch (1,18–11,36) in mehreren Gedankenschritten traktathaft abhandelt." See also pp 16–22.

[99] Wilckens 1982 (3) p 116.

on this point. While Barth, Nygren and Wilckens give a lot of attention to this problem, Cranfield does not. This does not imply that Cranfield fails to provide an answer to the problem; but the reader should bear in mind that Cranfield elaborates his answer less than the others.

Although Barth, Nygren, Cranfield and Wilckens express the theme of Romans in similar terms, they offer four different keys to the deeper understanding of this theme:

Barth: The key lies in the doctrine of the double predestination.
Nygren: The key lies in the idea of the two aeons.
Cranfield: The key lies in the moral relation between God and Man.
Wilckens: The key lies in the universal nature of the gospel.[100]

It is possible to recognize the keys from some of the constructive arguments found in the earlier analysis in this chapter. Constructive arguments were found earlier to support the choice of contextual arguments. Here we approach it from the opposite angle and can conclude that contextual arguments support constructive arguments, i e contextual arguments are related by complex means to the constructive assumptions. Barth, Nygren and Wilckens give different contextual arguments in support of their different views. Barth and Nygren pick out central or indicative passages of Romans. Barth points to 11:32 as the key to the understanding of Romans and Nygren starts from 5:12–21.[101] Wilckens refers to a much wider context, primarily Galatians.[102] Cranfield does not argue much for his belief that the key is to be found in the moral relation between God and Man.[103] Barth and Nygren thus refer to a more limited context than Wilckens.

Secondly, Nygren and Wilckens refer to historical arguments, which the others do not. Nygren points out that the thought-forms of Paul and his time differed from ours. Secularization creates problems for the modern reader when it comes to understanding Paul's two-aeon-thinking, according to

---

[100] Cf chapter three: 4. The theme of Romans.
[101] Barth 1926 p 407, where he writes in opposition to Lietzmann's view: "Wir wenden uns staunend ab, um festzustellen, daß wir es hier vielmehr mit dem grimmig beunruhigenden Axiom zu tun haben, in dem der Schlüssel des ganzen Römerbriefs (und nicht nur des Römerbriefs!) zu finden sein dürfte." Nygren 1944 p 213, 1952 p 207: "Here the whole problem of Romans is brought together in this brief passage that is filled to overflowing with vital thought."
[102] Wilckens 1978 (1) p 48: "Im Römerbrief wiederholt Paulus sie, jedoch nunmehr, wie oben gezeigt, zur Verantwortung seines Evangeliums unter dem – gegenüber dem Galaterbrief neuen – Thema der Einheit von Juden und Heiden", followed by a table of the parallel structures of Galatians and Romans. Cf p 89.
[103] See however Cranfield 1985 (1) p 88 n 3–4 concerning the progression of thought and structure of Romans.

Nygren.[104] Wilckens examines carefully Paul's historical circumstances. He refers to the threatened split in the church, which was a major concern of Paul's.[105] The Jerusalem collection was aimed at expressing the unity between the congregations which were influenced by Paul's theology and the centre of opposition to them, the Jerusalem congregation. The collection "sollte zu einem unübersehbaren Erweis jener Einheit von Juden und Heiden unter dem Evangelium werden, wie er sie in seinen Gemeinden verkündigte und praktizierte."[106] Thus, the conflict within the church had bearing also on the conflict between the two different religious groups.[107]

Thirdly, Barth, Cranfield and Wilckens offer important constructive arguments. Barth and Cranfield refer to the theological constructive argument of their images of God. To Barth God is "das ganz andere", while to Cranfield God is moral: "But for God simply to pass over sins would be altogether incompatible with His righteousness."[108] Cranfield and Wilckens give another theological comprehensive argument although they differ from each other in content. It concerns the essence of the gospel. Cranfield describes the gospel as effective power, which enables Christians to lead a new life and to obey God. Wilckens understands the essence of the gospel to be about the unity between Jews and Gentiles.[109]

Thus, we can conclude that a relation of dependence exists between contextual and constructive arguments, so that Barth's and Wilckens' different understandings of the key to the interpretation of the theme of Romans must be explained by reference to these combinations of contextual and constructive arguments. In Nygren's and Wilckens' commentaries the contextual arguments on this issue are combined with historical arguments.

Two reflections spring from this conclusion. First, since we have seen above that the same contextual arguments (supporting the interpretations of how Jesus Christ brought salvation to human beings) can be advanced in support of different interpretations, we must conclude that this kind of argument is necessary, but not sufficient for the interpretations and general remarks. Furthermore, when different contextual support is given for different

---

[104] Nygren 1944 pp 31f, 1952 pp 24f. It should also be noted that the way that exegetes have shown the importance of eschatology, i e a natural argument, is decisive for Nygren; 1944 p 17, 1952 p 9: "If there is anything which the newer exegetical study has clearly established, it is the extraordinary significance which the eschatological had for early Christian faith."

[105] Wilckens 1978 (1) pp 44–46.

[106] Wilckens 1978 (1) p 45.

[107] See Wilckens 1978 (1) pp 44–46 and 1982 (3) pp 128–130 and 131f (Zusammenfassung).

[108] Barth 1926 p 11 and Cranfield 1985 (1) pp 211f.

[109] Cranfield 1985 (1) pp 87f, 90 and 384 and Wilckens 1978 (1) p 85: "Das Evangelium negiert nicht nur den gesellschaftlichen Unterschied zwischen Griechen und Barbaren (1,14), sondern, für den jüdischen Aspekt noch ungleich radikaler, auch die heilsgeschichtliche διαστολὴ Ἰουδαίου τε καὶ ͨἝλληνος (10,12)."

interpretations, as here, it is necessary to ask what motivated the choice of contextual reference. Thus, contextual arguments are sufficient in neither case for the interpretation or understanding of Romans. Rather, contextual arguments need support from either historical or constructive arguments, which offer a clear guide as to which is the relevant context. Secondly, it is possible here to discern a problem concerning my earlier classification of Nygren's concept of the two aeons as a constructive assumption. Here it is clear that Nygren views this idea instead as a historical assumption. While I am aware that my classification does not correspond to Nygren's intentions, I would like nevertheless to keep my classification of two-aeon thinking as a constructive assumption. Further arguments in support of this interpretation of Nygren call for an account of his purposes which will be given in the next chapter.

Let us thus conclude this section by stating that Barth, Nygren, Cranfield and Wilckens cite different kinds of arguments also in connection with the general remarks. The contextual arguments are used either in the same form for different opinions (Paul's purpose) or in different forms for different opinions (the key to the understanding of the theme of Romans). However, alternative interpretations of the context, e g in the form of a consistency argument, are not found in the commentaries concerning these issues. It seems instead as if the decisive arguments are historical and constructive, as was most clear in relation to the general remarks on Paul's Jewish origin and the fundamental problem of Romans 14:1–15:13.

4. Conclusions

Two main conclusions can be drawn from this attempt to explain the different interpretations of Romans 7, some theological themes of Romans and the different general remarks on Romans found in the commentaries of Barth, Nygren, Cranfield and Wilckens.

The first main conclusion is that the differences in interpretation and general remarks cannot be explained by reference to the commentators' pursuit of certain kinds of interpretation or purpose of supporting their general remarks with arguments of a certain kind. Rather, they pursue different combinations of kinds of interpretations and arguments as well as combinations of reconstructive and constructive interpretations and arguments.

Let me begin with the difference between reconstructive and constructive interpretations. In the commentaries of Barth, Nygren, Cranfield and Wilckens, the different interpretations of the identity of ἐγώ and of some of the theological themes of Romans must be explained by reference both to reconstructive and constructive interpretations. Similarly, the differences in their general remarks must be explained by reference to arguments of both types.

In the case of the different combinations of kinds of interpretations and arguments, no simple model is employed in any of the commentaries. However, a pattern can be discerned for each commentary in two ways. First, some generalizations can be made concerning the combinations of the commentaries. In Barth's commentary constructive arguments dominate and are combined with contextual arguments and frequently also with other constructive arguments. In Nygren's commentary constructive arguments are also combined with other constructive arguments, but often with philological and contextual arguments as well. In Cranfield's commentary primarily philological, contextual and constructive arguments are combined. Finally, in Wilckens' commentary historical arguments are combined with a variety of arguments – philological, contextual, intentional and constructive.

However, this pattern becomes blurred when we consider that the commentators mostly mix these different kinds of arguments without taking account of their different characters. They follow no explicit methodological strategy. This lack of a clear methodological strategy carries an obvious risk, namely that any kind of argument is good as long as it supports the interpretation of the commentator. The huge variety of kinds of arguments on different issues conveys the impression that these commentators have not altogether succeeded in avoiding this danger with the possible exception of Barth, who has the smallest number of kinds of interpretations, mostly referring to constructive arguments. Although not setting out to deceive the reader, these commentators do not say why an argument of one kind is chosen at a specific point and not an argument of another kind.

A second generalization is however possible if the results of the analysis in this chapter are inspected more closely. Some arguments recur concerning the different issues analysed. Especially conspicuous are Barth's constructive arguments of the dualistic ontology, pessimistic anthropology and the double predestination, Nygren's constructive argument of the two aeons, Cranfield's constructive argument of the moral relation between God and Man and Wilckens' historical arguments of the situation of Paul and the church and the "Tun-Ergehen-Zusammenhang". Because of the frequency with which they occur, I have understood these recurring arguments as a kind of interpretive basis for each commentary. Thus, Barth's, Nygren's and Cranfield's commentaries have a constructive interpretive basis, while Wilckens' has a historical interpretive basis. Wilckens does not, however, as indicated above, refrain from constructive arguments; constructive arguments however do not constitute as clear a thematic basis in Wilckens as in the other commentaries.

Now, one problem these interpretive bases present is that they are not clearly related to the other type of interpretation in the commentaries. Reconstructive and constructive arguments are mostly treated as if they were on a par, of the same type. Since Barth's commentary is dominated by his interpretive basis, the problem is greater concerning Nygren's, Cranfield's and Wilckens' commentaries. What is the connection between Nygren's and Cranfield's constructive bases and their reconstructive arguments? The fact that Wilckens refrains from a constructive interpretive basis does not imply that he refrains from constructive arguments: he is therefore open to the same question about the connection between the two types of arguments.

Our second main conclusion concerns the character of the different kinds of arguments. This analysis provides material for reflection on how the different kinds of arguments function. The philological arguments put forward in this chapter are both taken as support for opposite opinions (the identity of ἐγώ and how Jesus Christ brought salvation to human beings). Philological arguments thus provide insufficient support for an interpretation or a general remark. The choice of meaning of a philological argument must be explained by reference to other kinds of arguments. The same is true of the contextual arguments. The same argument is taken to support opposing views and different arguments support different interpretations. The contextual arguments are frequent and the interpreter's difficulties in finding contextual support for his interpretation constitute no problem. Thus, neither contextual arguments provide a sufficient basis for the choice of an interpretation or a general remark.

The historical arguments however constitute a clearer point of departure. Although Wilckens' arguments for a cultic interpretation of God's work in Christ do not rule out other possibilities, his historical argument provides a sufficient basis for his interpretation.

The intentional arguments are by their nature difficult to assess. Obviously neither Nygren, Cranfield nor Wilckens had any difficulty referring to Paul's intentions concerning the purpose of Romans. However none of them can prove that they are right and the context obviously allows for opposing possibilities. Intentional arguments do not provide a sufficient basis for the choice of interpretation, since it is impossible to analyse Paul's intentions, what was in his mind when writing Romans.

The natural arguments do not appear very important. Although references to authorities and scholars are frequent, they seldom constitute a real argument.

With the exception of the interpretation of the identity of ἐγώ, consistency arguments are not given. In principle they offer an opportunity to come to terms with the weaknesses of the philological, contextual and intentional arguments. They provide an additional criterion which forces the interpreter to take conflicting contexts into account. These commentators scarcely avail themselves of this opportunity.

Instead, the constructive arguments often prove decisive, particularly in the interpretations and general remarks of Barth, Nygren and Cranfield. Logically they precede the choice of philological, contextual and intentional support. As we have seen, a clear constructive basis may be discerned for these commentaries. The constructive arguments are also decisive in Wilckens' commentary, but are balanced there by the historical arguments, which constitute the interpretive basis of his commentary.

Thus, some explanation of the different interpretations and general remarks is possible by reference to the different kinds of supporting arguments. First, these four commentaries all refer to constructive arguments allowing for text-external assumptions in the interpretation process. In this way the opportunities for different interpretations increase in comparison to interpretations and general remarks based on reconstructive arguments. Secondly, the differences can be explained by reference to the commentators' different combinations of arguments. Each commentary has its own dominating combination of arguments, which differs from the others'. Thirdly, each commentator has an interpretive basis, which is characteristic for his commentary. Fourthly, the historical and constructive arguments, which constitute the commentators' different bases of interpretation, are kinds of arguments which have the characteristic of being decisive for the choice of interpretation. This characteristic is not shared by the other arguments used. Therefore, the different contents of the commentators' interpretive bases to a large extent explain the variations between Barth's, Nygren's, Cranfield's and Wilckens' interpretations of Romans.

Chapter Five

The Purposes of the Commentaries

In this chapter I shall consider whether the differences between the commentaries' interpretations of Romans and their different understandings of the general remarks can be explained by their pursuit of different purposes.[1] I shall also examine whether the commentators' purposes coincide with the results they arrive at. In order to characterize the purposes of Barth's, Nygren's, Cranfield's and Wilckens' commentaries I differentiate between six kinds of purposes, which have been derived from the commentaries. I focus on a fundamental difference between these purposes by distinguishing between critical and creative purposes. The commentaries are characterized in relation to these two ways of distinguishing their purposes. Thereafter I offer some explanations of the differences.

In order to examine whether the purposes of the commentaries coincide with their results I relate the kinds of purposes to the two fundamental types of interpretation, reconstructive and constructive interpretation, referred to in chapter four. Then I compare the results of this analysis with the purposes intended by Barth, Nygren, Cranfield and Wilckens.

1. The purposes of the commentaries

The purposes of the commentaries relate to different levels. At least six purposes can be discerned:

(a) to clarify the original meaning of the text,
(b) to reconstruct the historical situation when Romans was written,
(c) to clarify Paul's theology,
(d) to examine critically theological points of view on the basis of the interpretation of the text,
(e) to resolve present-day problems of the church, and
(f) to express Christian faith today.[2]

The difference between (a), to clarify the original meaning of the text, and (b), to reconstruct the historical situation when Romans was written, con-

[1] The idea that differences in interpretation are due to differences of purpose is put forward in many works on the theory of interpretation, see e g Hermerén 1982, Olsson 1984 and Morgan with Barton 1988 pp 5–15.
[2] The categories are inspired by Hermerén 1982 and Olsson 1984.

cerns the prime focus. (a) concentrates on the text and (b) on the historical situation presupposed in the text. (c), to clarify Paul's theology, aims at dealing with the contents of Romans in a more systematic way, setting out recurring themes, while going less into detail. Thus (a) differs from (c) in being less systematic and going more into detail. Note the restricted meaning of "theology" here.[3] (d) differs from (a), (b) and (c) in not focusing on the text, but examining the history of theology in the light of the critical interpretation of the text. (d) differs from (e) and (f) in not aiming at the development of the author's theological views. There is also a difference between (e) and (f). The purpose of resolving present-day problems of the church (e) is more pragmatic, but at the same time less comprehensive than that of expressing Christian faith today (f). (e) is not however to be understood as purely pragmatic; it embraces theoretical considerations as well.

Cranfield is the only one of these authors who clearly seeks to avoid exceeding the limits of exegesis proper. I have taken his demarcation to be a rejection of the purpose of resolving present-day problems of the church (e) and expressing Christian faith today (f). Instead he puts a great deal of effort into clarifying the original meaning of the text (a). He also aims to distinguish between purpose (a) on the one hand and (c), clarification of Paul's theology on the other, and therefore intends to reserve (c) for the essays.[4]

Barth, Nygren and Wilckens also take present-day problems, (e) and (f), into consideration and do not limit their analyses as Cranfield does. Barth indeed keeps close to the detail of the text, but pays hardly any attention to its original meaning (a) or to the historical situation (b). Barth focuses on the expression of Christian faith today (f) by clarifying Paul's theology (c).[5] This

---

[3] Cf the introduction to chapter two.
[4] Cranfield 1985 (1) p 1: "Judging the proper function of the introduction to a commentary to be to furnish the reader with such information as will enable him to approach the detailed exegesis efficiently but with a still open mind rather than to present him with the commentator's ready-made answers to all important questions (in our view, an illegitimate procedure(...)), we have decided to place both our general discussion of the theology of Romans and also our discussion of the difficult question of Paul's purpose or purposes in writing it not in the introduction but in volume two at the end of the exegetical notes." See p ix for the same wary attitude concerning the translation of the Greek text. On p 37 Cranfield rejects any purpose going beyond the "natural meaning" of the text and stresses the importance of giving an account of alternative interpretations. Cf p 68, where Cranfield rejects an interpretation as "doctrinaire".
[5] Barth 1926 p viii: "Dieses Buch will nichts anderes sein als ein Stück des Gesprächs eines Theologen mit Theologen." Concerning the limits of historical-critical exegesis, Barth writes: "...Paulus zu *verstehen* d. h. aufzudecken, wie das, was dasteht, nicht nur griechisch oder deutsch irgendwie nachgesprochen sondern nach-*gedacht* werden, wie es etwa *gemeint* sein könnte", p x. Further, p xi on the modern application, Barth refers to Calvin, who was working with Romans "bis die Mauer zwischen dem 1. und 16. Jahrhundert *transparent* wird, bis Paulus dort *redet* und der Mensch des 16. Jahrhunderts hier *hört*, bis das Gespräch zwischen Urkunde und Leser ganz auf die *Sache* (die hier und dort keine verschiedene sein *kann*!) konzentriert ist."

makes Barth's commentary clearly different from Nygren's. Nygren is less interested in the detail level, but focuses on the original meaning of the text (a), systematized into the theology of Paul (c), which according to Nygren implies the expression of Christian faith today (f).[6]

Wilckens' purposes, finally, are to clarify the original meaning of the text (a), to reconstruct historically the situation at the time Romans was written (b), to clarify Paul's theology (c), to examine critically theological points of view on the basis of interpretation of the text (d) and to resolve present-day problems of the church (e), defined by Wilckens as the ecumenical problem of the division between the Protestant and Catholic churches. It should be noted that in this purpose Wilckens focuses on the overcoming of theological conflicts and that (d) mainly concerns the conflict between Catholic and Protestant theology.[7] There is thus a similarity between Nygren's commentary and Wilckens' in that both draw on historical support to resolve present-day problems. The purposes of clarifying the original meaning of the text (a) and reconstructing the historical situation at the time Romans was written (b) are two different ways of relating what the text means today to what it once

---

[6] Nygren 1944 p 34, 1952 p 27: "It will pay us best to give open-minded attention to what Paul actually says, rather than to thoughts of our own that may be awakened by what he says. The distraction of associations that may cling to words removed from their context must be avoided. Step by step we must resolutely follow Paul's thought and observe as he builds up his message. The individual declarations cannot otherwise be understood, for they depend for their meaning on the context which they serve" and 1944 p 11, 1952 p 3: "What the gospel is, what the content of Christian faith is, one learns to know in the Epistle to the Romans as in no other place in the New Testament. Romans gives us the gospel in its wide context. It gives us the right perspective and the standard by which we should comprehend all the constituent parts of the Gospels, to arrive at the true, intended picture."

[7] For (a) see e g the structure of Wilckens' commentary. Each section begins with an "Analyse", which goes into the details of the text. For (b) see e g 1978 (1) pp 33–41, cf above chapter two e g on the relation between the covenants and on how Jesus Christ brought salvation to human beings. Concerning (c), Wilckens clearly states, in contrast to Cranfield, the central theological message of Paul already in the introduction, p vi: "... Versöhnung als Aufhebung aller Entfremdung durch Gottes Kraft im Kreuz Christi. Von daher ist christliches, an Paulus geschultes Denken selbst in seiner Struktur geprägt; (...) Wer im Durchgang durch den Römerbrief gewahr wird, wie alle Gedankenlinien des Paulus auf das 'ingens miraculum' dieses Geschehens in Tod und Auferstehung Christi zulaufen und so die begriffliche Struktur seiner ganzen Denkbewegung ein Umdenken in dieser Richtung fordert und ermöglicht, ..." Cf the frequent references to the theme of "iustificatio impii", e g pp 166, 330 and 1980 (2) p 258. Concerning (d) see Wilckens 1978 (1) p 52: "Der vorliegende Kommentar möchte dazu einen Beitrag geben, indem er die alttestamentlich-jüdische Fundierung der paulinischen Rechtfertigungslehre so herauszuarbeiten sucht, daß von diesem historischen Geschichtspunkt aus die entscheidenden Kontroverspunkte der konfessionellen Wirkungsgeschichte des Textes gemeinsam aufgearbeitet werden können." For examples see pp 250–257 (Zusammenfassung), 300–305 (Zusammenfassung) and 1980 (2) pp 22–33 (Zusammenfassung). Concerning (e), 1978 (1) p vi: "Mir will scheinen, daß der Römerbrief, über dem vor allem unsere Kirchen auseinandergebrochen sind, konsequent historisch-kritisch ausgelegt, auch die wirkungsgeschichtlich-kritische Kraft gewinnt, sie am entscheidenden Punkt heute wieder in die Einheit zurückzurufen, die der historische Römerbrief zu seiner Zeit bewirken wollte." See also pp 142–146 (excursus).

meant in the original historical situation. A table will summarize conclusions
so far:

	Barth	Nygren	Cranfield	Wilckens
Original meaning		a	a	a
Historical situation				b
Paul's theology	c	c	c	c
Critical examination				d
Present-day problems				e
Faith today	f	f		

It is possible intuitively to discern a difference between purposes (a)–(d) on
the one hand and (e) and (f) on the other. This difference arises because the
Bible is both an object of academic study and a norm in the believing communities.[8] As Morgan says, the Bible is both involved in the study of religion and
in the process of doing theology.[9]

First, purposes (a)–(c) involve the description, analysis and explanation of
the text, while (e) and (f) are concerned with its application. (d) constitutes
an intermediate link, but takes its point of departure in (a)–(c). Secondly,
while (a)–(d) can be pursued by anyone, Christian or not, (e) and (f) fall
within the sphere of faith. This implies not only that (e) and (f) involve a belief in the existence of God and a belief that the Bible is God's Word, but also
that the interpretation of the biblical text is related to certain assumptions
about God, mankind, the world etc, that is, a set of Christian beliefs. Consequently, as far as purposes (e) and (f) are concerned, arguments are valid
which cannot be accepted in respect of purposes (a)–(d), where the arguments must be acceptable, at least in principle, to those who do not share the
Christian faith. Purposes (e) and (f) rely on personal convictions, which go
beyond the limits of strictly rational reasoning. Thirdly, the results of purposes (a)–(d) are hypothetical in character, while the results of purposes (e) and
(f) are normative. It is in the nature of academic studies that the results remain open to discussion.

I call purposes (a)–(d) *critical* purposes and purposes (e) and (f) *creative*.
Describing, analysing and explaining the content and/or historical context of
a text are critical purposes as is the critical examination of theological points
of view on the basis of the (critical) interpretation of the text.[10] On the other
hand, the statement of theological points of view on the basis of the critical
interpretation of the text concerning God, mankind, the world etc is a creative
purpose.

[8] Cf Barr 1981b pp 36f.
[9] Morgan with Barton 1988 p 167. Cf Holte 1984 pp 39–41 and his distinction between theology 1 and theology 2.
[10] The different purposes will be related to the different interpretations in the next section.

We can conclude from the above analysis that Cranfield's commentary has only critical purposes, while Barth's, Nygren's and Wilckens' commentaries have both critical and creative purposes. The creative purposes may be more or less inclusive. Solving the present-day problems of the church (e) is a limited creative purpose. Thus, Wilckens' creative purpose is more limited than Barth's or Nygren's.

The results of the critical purposes are allowed to bear on the creative purposes in varying degree. A commentary may be predominantly critical or predominantly creative. Let me characterize the commentaries by establishing the way in which they combine their purposes in terms of critical and creative purposes and by analysing how these purposes are related to one another.

The purpose of Barth's commentary is primarily the creative one of expressing Christian faith today (f). His critical purpose of clarifying Paul's theology (c) is clearly subordinated to the creative purpose.[11] Nygren combines the critical purposes of clarifying the original meaning of the text (a) and clarifying Paul's theology (c) with the creative purpose of stating theological points of view on the basis of the interpretations of Romans (f). Nygren claims that the critical purpose forms the basis for the creative purpose. He further holds these purposes to be closely related to one another. Expressing Paul's theology is the same as expressing Christian faith today.[12] Cranfield combines the two critical purposes of clarifying the original meaning of the text (a) and clarifying Paul's theology (c). His intention is to differentiate between the two by the structural device of leaving conclusions concerning the theology of Romans until the final essay "Concluding remarks on some aspects of the theology of Romans".[13] Wilckens combines the four kinds of critical purposes (a)–(d) with the creative purpose of solving the ecumenical problem. He states that the critical purposes are the basis of the creative purpose.[14]

Thus, Barth subordinates his critical purpose to his creative purpose. Nygren assumes a close relation between his critical purpose and the creative purpose. Cranfield intends to keep the two critical purposes apart. Finally,

[11] See also Barth 1926 p xix in the introduction to the third edition, where he writes that commentaries on Romans must be written over and over again, since times change, implying that his primary purpose is (f). His creative purpose is also indicated by his use of the first person plural, thus directly addressing the readers, see e g pp 68–74.

[12] Cf above this chapter n 6.

[13] Cf above this chapter n 4 and Cranfield 1986 (2) pp 823–870.

[14] Cf above this chapter n 7 and Wilckens 1978 (1) p 52: "Der vorliegende Kommentar möchte dazu einen Beitrag geben, indem er die alttestamentlich-jüdische Fundierung der paulinischen Rechtfertigungslehre so herauszuarbeiten sucht, daß von diesem historischen Geschichtspunkt aus die entscheidenden Kontroverspunkte der konfessionellen Wirkungsgeschichte des Textes gemeinsam aufgearbeitet werden können. So könnte gerade der ehemals so umstrittene, konfessionelle Zwietracht legitimierende Römerbrief in unserer Gegenwart bewirken, was er in seiner Zeit bewirken wollte: zur Einheit der Kirche zu provozieren."

Wilckens subordinates his creative purpose to his critical purposes. On a scale from predominantly critical to predominantly creative, we can arrange the commentaries in this order: Cranfield, Wilckens, Nygren and Barth.

These different purposes of the commentaries and their different relations within each commentary may offer some explanation for the differences between the interpretations and general remarks put forward in the commentaries. If we focus on Barth's prime creative purpose and Cranfield's and Wilckens' prime critical purposes and consider that Nygren's close relation between the critical and creative purposes makes his commentary more like Barth's commentary than Cranfield's and Wilckens', the differences in interpretations and general remarks can be explained in the following ways.

With respect, first, to the interpretation of Paul's law-concept in Romans 7, Cranfield's and Wilckens' critical purposes may explain why they interpret the law as the Mosaic law. In the same way, Barth and Nygren, pursuing primarily creative goals, interpret Paul as having a wider concept of the law. According to Barth and Nygren, the law is a kind of universal, theological category. It should also be noted that Wilckens' secondary creative purpose does not affect his interpretation of the law.[15]

The same may be seen concerning the interpretation of the theological theme of the relation between the two covenants, where Barth and Nygren interpret the old covenant as a universal theological category and Cranfield and Wilckens interpret it as God's covenant with Israel. The difference between Nygren's critical purpose on the one hand and Cranfield's and Wilckens' on the other also becomes clear in respect of this issue. Nygren's critical purpose does not exclude a theological interpretation of the identity of the old covenant, while for Cranfield and Wilckens it does.[16] Thus, Nygren's closer relation between his critical and creative purposes as compared with Wilckens' is evident. It is also clear from his interpretation of Paul's view of atonement that Wilckens gives priority to the critical purpose.[17] Wilckens critically examines Anselm's satisfaction doctrine on the basis of a description of Paul's view.

As to the general remarks on Romans, the different purposes can explain some of the differences. Barth's and Nygren's creative purpose explains their lack of interest in the situation of the Romans as a means to obtain a correct understanding of the epistle and Cranfield's and Wilckens' critical purposes explain why they take the opposite view.[18] The same difference concerning the critical purposes of Nygren on the one hand and Cranfield and Wilckens on the other can be seen in their different understandings of Paul's Jewish ori-

---

[15] Cf chapter one: 2. The law.
[16] Cf chapter two: 1. The old covenant, the character of God and the need for salvation.
[17] Cf pp 40 f.
[18] Cf chapter three: 2. The Romans and Paul's opponents.

gin. Cranfield points to Paul's dependence on the Old Testament and Wilckens to his dependence on the apocalyptic tradition. However, Nygren starts from a description of the Pharisees, but focuses on the theological meaning – that Paul knows both ways to salvation. Wilckens' critical purposes are shown int al in the way he brings out the point that Paul's apostleship was questioned and that he feared developments in church politics would lead to a split in the church.[19]

One striking link between the different purposes of the commentaries and their general remarks on the epistle is the similarity between the commentators' purposes and the purposes ascribed to Paul. According to Barth and Nygren, Paul's purpose was to expound contemporary Christianity and according to Wilckens, his purpose was to resolve a specific problem of the church. Cranfield holds that Paul's purpose was to present his gospel because of his missionary plans.[20] This might lead one to suppose that Cranfield's purpose does not correspond to the purpose ascribed to Paul, since Cranfield's purpose is not to expound Christianity today. That is mistaken, however, as will be clarified by the following conclusion drawn from the distinction between critical and creative purposes.

Some more general conclusions can be drawn from the distinction between the critical and creative purposes of the commentaries. In the case of the theological themes, the distinction between critical and creative purposes shows that theological matters can be dealt with not just by commentaries with creative purposes, like Barth's and Nygren's, but also by commentaries with critical purposes, like Cranfield's, although it has to be expected that there will be differences in their treatment of or approach to the theological themes. Likewise, in the case of the general remarks, it is not just the commentaries with critical purposes, like Cranfield's, that can bring to the fore aspects of the original meaning of the text; commentaries with creative purposes can also have the critical purpose of stating the original meaning of the text, like Nygren's. These two facts explain why characterizing the commentaries as either critical or creative, as is sometimes done, although often in more evaluative terms as "historical" or "doctrinal", is not enough. Let us however use the vague terms "historical" and "theological" for this difference in approach for the moment.

A commentary with a clear historical approach does not necessarily have to steer clear of theological matters. There is no contradiction in writing a commentary with critical purposes and having a creative purpose as well, so long as the two are kept apart and the relation between them is clear to the reader. Nygren's and Wilckens' commentaries clearly have this double purpose.

[19] Cf chapter three: 1. The apostle Paul.
[20] Cf chapter three: 3. The purpose and character of Romans.

However, none of the commentaries makes the relation between the two kinds of purposes clear to the reader, as we have seen in Nygren's commentary on the one hand and Cranfield's and Wilckens' on the other. Nygren allows for much more in his critical analyses than Cranfield and Wilckens. The line between the historical and the theological level is blurred.

Wilckens further claims that his creative purpose is subordinated to his critical purposes. There are however examples in his commentary which point the other way. Wilckens' creative purpose of contributing to a solution to the problem of the theological disagreements of the divided church partly explains his interpretations of some main points of conflict between the Catholic and Protestant churches as represented in the text of Romans, e g his interpretation of Paul's view of how human beings obtain righteousness. Wilckens wants neither to exclude the sola fide view nor the importance of good works.[21] Here the creative purpose of recalling the church to theological unity (e) seems to have influenced critical purposes (a)–(d) and not the other way about.

Thus, the commentators' pursuit of different goals explains some of the differences of interpretation and general remarks. However, we have seen that the purposes of the commentaries are not unproblematically related to what the commentators are actually doing. By relating the characterization of the commentaries' critical and creative purposes to the two fundamental types of interpretation from chapter four, we have an analysis instrument which takes us further into the examination of this difference between explicitly stated purposes and the actual results achieved by the commentators.

2. The results achieved by the commentaries

In saying that critical purposes are not compatible with arguments which presuppose the Christian faith, I have already intimated that the relation between the two types of purposes and the two types of interpretations is close. In other words, critical purposes are only compatible with reconstructive interpretations, since constructive interpretations are supported by references to assumptions which presuppose the Christian faith. On the other hand, creative purposes require also constructive arguments. When, for example, in interpreting the identity of ἐγώ in Romans 7, the interpreter concludes that the philological and contextual references are compatible with different interpretations, he assumes the Christian anthropology of the renewal of the Christian through the Spirit in a way that makes him or her essentially free

---

[21] Cf p 45. See also e g Wilckens 1978 (1) pp 223–233, in the excursus " 'Gerechtigkeit Gottes' 5. Die Gerechtigkeit Gottes in der Paulusexegese" on the interpretation of the righteousness of God.

from sin, and concludes that ἐγώ in Romans 7 cannot be the Christian.

Consequently, the different purposes pursued by Barth, Nygren, Cranfield and Wilckens and the relations they intend to keep between them mean that Barth stresses the constructive interpretations, Nygren draws on reconstructive interpretations for constructive interpretations, Cranfield refrains from constructive interpretations and Wilckens finds the basis for his constructive interpretations in his reconstructive interpretations. How does my description of the commentators' purposes accord with the results of the analysis of their fundamental types of interpretation in chapter four? It should be noted that this analysis is not an explanation of the results in chapter four. Rather, I use the results in chapter four as a means to explain the differences found in chapters one, two and three. This will be clear also from the fact that the references given in this chapter are not restricted to the references given in chapter four. The issues brought out have been chosen so as best to illuminate the problem of whether they achieve their goals. Since the point is less the comparison than the reasoning of each author, I have kept them separate.

The analysis in chapter four showed that all the authors make constructive interpretations. This implies that Cranfield does not achieve his purpose of being purely critical. The contents of his constructive arguments clearly indicate the assumptions he makes: God is righteous and severe. The proper attitude of Man toward God is obedience. Consequently, the law is good. Salvation establishes the good law and makes it possible for the Christian to fulfil it. Cranfield fulfils both critical and creative purposes. How are they interrelated? I will cite some examples from chapter four to clarify this relation.

Cranfield interprets the new covenant as having the same purposes of faith and obedience as the old, the old covenant having established the necessary conditions for the appearance of the new.[22] On the basis of Cranfield's critical purposes one might conclude that if constructive assumptions existed, they would not be decisive for the interpretation, but they are.

The constructive interpretation of the relation between the covenants is based on various contextual arguments. One of the most important arguments concerns 10:4 and after discussing various interpretations Cranfield concludes: "but we are convinced that there is no statement in any of Paul's epistles which, rightly understood, implies that Christ has abolished the law."[23] Then follows a survey of the corpus paulinum, where Cranfield, when confronted with the alternatives, invariably selects the interpretation that accords with his conviction. What criterion does Cranfield apply to decide whether the context has been "rightly understood"? My analysis shows that it

[22] pp 81 f.
[23] Cranfield 1986 (2) p 519, see also pp 516–518 and 853 (essays).

is to be found in the constructive arguments which set out the moral relation between God and Man. However, they do not seem to follow from the contextual arguments. They are raised, for example, in the introduction to 3:21–26 and contain both the picture of God and the anthropology.[24]

Thus, the two different types of purposes are pursued, but the author does not differentiate clearly between them. The contextual and constructive arguments are used as arguments of equal value. A generous interpretation of Cranfield would be to say that he regards the content of the constructive arguments as following from the historical analysis of Jewish thought as found in the Old Testament passages to which Paul refers.[25] However, Cranfield's interpretation of the relation between the covenants does not just imply that this is a correct description of Jewish thought and the background to Paul's thinking. It also implies that this is the way Paul understood Christianity – which is different. That reading requires a comparison of different Christian traditions. Cranfield seems here to be drawing on a tradition, in which God and Man are understood mainly in moral terms. His interpretation of the relation between the new and the old covenants is logically dependent on this theological assumption.

Nor is the connection between the reconstructive and the constructive interpretations kept clear in respect of Cranfield's interpretation of how Jesus Christ brought salvation to human beings. For example, when Cranfield interprets the word ἱλαστήριον in 3:25, he uses contextual arguments from the Old Testament to argue that it has a clear connection with God's wrath. This interpretation conflicts with those of many other exegetes to which Cranfield refers. What argument does Cranfield put forward for choosing this interpretation against the opinion of other scholars? His interpretation relies on the constructive argument of the moral relation between God and human beings.[26] The importance and conclusive nature of this constructive argument emerges still more clearly, for example, in the interpretation of 5:10 and in the concluding essay, where it is put forward without any supporting contextual arguments, rather as a self-evident presupposition for the interpretation of the atonement.[27] It is remarkable that a commentator whose intention to give only reconstructive interpretations is so clear should so openly take theological assumptions as his starting point.

It is thus difficult to argue that the key to the interpretation of the theme of

[24] Cranfield 1985 (1) p 200.
[25] Cranfield 1986 (2) pp 848f (essays).
[26] Cf p 86. See also Cranfield 1985 (1) pp 214–217, especially p 217: "We take it that what Paul's statement that God purposed Christ as a propitiatory victim means is that God, because in His mercy He willed to forgive sinful men and, being truly merciful, willed to forgive them righteously, that is, without in any way condoning their sin, purposed to direct against His own very Self in the person of His Son the full weight of that righteous wrath which they deserved."
[27] Cranfield 1985 (1) pp 267f and 1986 (2) pp 827f (essays).

justification through faith, i e the moral relation between God and Man, is derived purely from reconstructive interpretations in Cranfield's commentary. Though he gives contextual support for this key,[28] and states that his interpretation is in accordance with the Old Testament texts,[29] he reveals his own commitment to the moral interpretation by suddenly referring to his readers in the first person plural. On "the meaning of the believer's liberation"[30] in 8:4 Cranfield writes that: "The law's requirement will be fulfilled by the determination of the direction, the set, of our lives by the Spirit, by our being enabled again and again to decide for the Spirit and against the flesh. . ."[31] Furthermore, his view of the key to the understanding of Romans is supported by several other constructive arguments concerning the image of God and the essence of the gospel.[32]

Thus, Cranfield does not fulfil his purpose of analysing the content of Romans only in critical terms, but gives also constructive arguments. These neither follow from the reconstructive interpretations, nor are they parentheses or found in the essays. The constructive arguments are prerequisites if Cranfield's interpretations are to be tenable. Remarkably enough, this fundamental point of departure is not made explicit. On the contrary, Cranfield denies theological assumptions. As a consequence, Cranfield makes his readers think his interpretations are strictly reconstructive, which is false. Further, the connection between these theological and anthropological assumptions on the one hand and the different kinds of reconstructive arguments on the other becomes blurred. Although frequently used, the constructive arguments are not admitted as arguments of a different character.

One more thing should be noticed concerning Cranfield's two critical purposes. Cranfield aims to reserve the descriptions of Paul's theology for the concluding essays of his commentary. However, he states bluntly there that he will not give a full account of the theology found in the epistle, because it would involve "a great deal of tiresome repetition of things already said in the commentary."[33] Cranfield does not fulfil his purposes in this respect either.

In accordance with his prime creative purpose, Barth makes constructive interpretations all the way, as can be seen from the analysis in chapter four. Does Barth fulfil his creative purpose? As with Cranfield, there is no difficulty finding the content of Barth's constructive assumptions in his arguments. They reveal a pessimistic anthropology, a dualistic ontology and a special doctrine of the double predestination, according to which all are predestined

---

[28] E g Cranfield 1985 (1) p 88 n 4, see also pp 96–99.
[29] Cranfield 1985 (1) p 384.
[30] Cranfield 1985 (1) p 383.
[31] Cranfield 1985 (1) p 385.
[32] Cf p 99.
[33] Cranfield 1986 (2) p 824 (essays). He does not actually refrain from throwing light on today's problems in the church either, cf p 628 on diaconal work.

both to damnation and salvation. How is all this related to Barth's critical purpose of clarifying Paul's theology?

According to Barth, the new covenant is the synthesis of the old covenant and its opposite.[34] This interpretation is supported by the dualistic ontology. Since the old covenant is human, it is alien to God.[35] The pattern of dialectical philosophy is also used in expressions like "unsre Religion besteht in der Aufhebung unsrer Religion" and the statement that redeemed man "lebt von der *Negation* der Negation".[36] That these constructive arguments are (logical) points of departure rather than derived from an analysis of the text of Romans, is clear, for example, from Barth's habit of making clarifying additions in his translations[37] or, as in the case of 3:1–20, giving them already in the introduction.[38]

It becomes clear from Barth's interpretation of the characteristics of Christian life that the dualistic ontology preceded both his anthropology and his doctrine of the double predestination. Since the divine reality is opposed to human reality, the picture of human life becomes pessimistic and it is evident that if men are to be able to obtain peace with God a condemnation is necessary. But if all are condemned how is salvation possible?[39] The same constructive arguments are used also to interpret the characteristics of Christian life. Their character of basic presuppositions is clear. Barth holds that dialectical thinking is natural, when pondering on life.[40] The idea of God on the other side of the ontological abyss is based on the concept of God itself, according to Barth. God cannot be God if he is only one possibility among others. The ultimate truth of human life belongs to the divine sphere, beyond the limits of human control.[41] Thus, on the one hand, some of Barth's assumptions are held by him to be self-evident either from experience or from the definition of concepts. On the other hand, truth is ultimately concealed beyond human

---

[34] p 81.

[35] Barth 1926 p 62.

[36] Barth 1926 pp 84 and 180.

[37] E g on 5:16–17 Barth 1926 pp 154f (Barth's additions are in italics and are also marked in his commentary): "Und *da ist* nicht *Gleichgewicht, so daß man sagen könnte*: Wie das durch den einen Sünder *in die Welt* Gekommene, so das Geschenk, *das durch den einen Gerechten den Menschen gegeben ist.* (Denn *darin ist das Verhältnis allerdings parallel*: das Gericht wurde, bei einem Menschen einsetzend, zum Todesurteil, die Begnadung aber, bei vieler *Menschen* Fall einsetzend, zur Gerechtsprechung). Denn *(und das ist die Aufhebung der Parallele)* wenn im Fall des Einen *und* durch diesen Einen der Tod zur Königsherrschaft gelangte, so werden um so gewisser die, welche die Fülle der Gnade und die Gabe der Gerechtigkeit empfangen, selber Könige werden im Leben durch den Einen: Jesus Christus."

[38] Barth 1926 pp 51f, which contains both the dualistic ontology and the dialectial synthesis.

[39] Barth 1926 pp 295–297 and 416–418.

[40] Barth 1926 p 411.

[41] Barth 1926 p 297: "Wie könnte sie die Wahrheit sein, wenn wir, wie wir sind, direkte Einsicht von ihr nehmen könnten? Wie könnte sie Gott sein, wenn sie uns je eine Möglichkeit unter andern werden könnte?"

reach. On this issue, too, the constructive interpretations thus form clear points of departure, as may be seen for example in the additions Barth makes in his translation of 12:2, where he strengthens the opposite ways of life by the additions of "bestehende" and "kommende", indicating not only future fulfilment, but also its contradictory relation to the present.[42] On 12:16 Barth states bluntly: "*Wir* stehen *tiefer* im Nein als im Ja. Wir möchten das Verständnis für diese *Störung* des Gleichgewichts der Lebensbetrachtung geradezu als conditio sine qua non für das Verständnis des Römerbriefs und seiner Botschaft aufstellen."[43] Men's opposition to the divine reality, their condemnation and the ambiguity of life are clear.

In the problem discussed in 14:1–15:13 Barth sees an example of his constructive basis. Neither the weak nor the strong are right, since all that is human is unclean in the sight of God.[44] To live a proper Christian life means constantly remembering the double predestination: all that is human is condemned and all that is human is ultimately saved in the transcendent reality.[45]

Thus Barth's ontological, anthropological and theological assumptions constitute the interpretive basis that shapes the whole of his interpretation. The constructive interpretations dominate the reconstructive interpretations. This is clear from the actual comments on each issue, but it is also explicitly stated in the introduction: "Wenn ich ein 'System' habe, so besteht es darin, daß ich das, was Kierkegaard den 'unendlichen qualitativen Unterschied' von Zeit und Ewigkeit genannt hat, in seiner negativen und positiven Bedeutung möglichst beharrlich im Auge behalte. 'Gott ist im Himmel und du auf Erden'. Die Beziehung *dieses* Gottes zu *diesem* Menschen, die Beziehung *dieses* Menschen zu *diesem* Gott ist für mich das Thema der Bibel und die Summe der Philosophie in Einem."[46] Barth fulfils his explicit creative purpose of expressing Christian faith today from a clearly stated point of departure. Barth's critical purpose of clarifying Paul's theology is subordinated to the creative purpose to the degree that expressions of the constructive assumptions are found in Barth's translations. This makes the relations between Barth's constructive interpretations and the text problematic. Barth brushes against the borderline between interpretation and penning a new text. I find it difficult, nevertheless, to argue that Barth's commentary is not an interpretation of Romans. An interpretation of a text made with clear points of departure re-

---

[42] Barth 1926 p 410.
[43] Barth 1926 p 446.
[44] Cf p 93. Barth 1926 p 498: "Sobald und sofern für Gott und seine Freiheit der Mensch und seine 'Frömmigkeit' substituiert wird, bedeutet seine Haltung, welche sie auch sei, Verwerfung." See also p 501.
[45] Barth 1926 pp 487 and 496–498.
[46] Barth 1926 p xiii.

mains an interpretation of the text. It is only when the connection between text, constructive assumptions and interpretation is blurred that the border-line is in danger of being crossed. One problem connected with Barth's commentary is his contradictory claim that the constructive assumptions are self-evident and thus true, while truth belongs totally to the divine and hidden sphere. Barth is aware of the problem, but takes the view that this does not relieve people of the necessity to seek the truth, although we need to be aware that we can never attain it and that all expressions of faith are parables.[47]

Nygren claims to make reconstructive interpretations on which his constructive interpretations are based. The content of the constructive arguments is almost entirely confined to the idea of the two aeons in its theological, onto-logical and anthropological senses.[48] Contained in its theological and onto-logical meanings is the idea that God has overcome the four forces of destruction with his agape. Contained in its anthropological meaning is the idea that Christian life is lived within these two aeons. Does Nygren fulfil his purposes? What then is the connection between Nygren's critical and creative purposes?

In our discussion of the key to the interpretation of the theme of Romans in chapter four, we concluded that Nygren himself would not agree that the idea of the two aeons should be classified as a constructive argument. Instead, he classifies it as a historical argument.[49] Thus, the problem of the interpretation of Nygren's idea of the two aeons strikes at the relation between Nygren's re-constructive and constructive interpretations.

Nygren claims that the idea of the two aeons has a reconstructive inter-pretive basis and supports this with contextual and intentional arguments in addition to the historical argument that Paul's thought-forms differ from ours.[50] The contextual arguments are given on three levels. First, a central section is indicated (5:12–21), which is given prominence on the basis of its abrupt appearance and axiomatic character.[51] Secondly, this idea is said to re-cur throughout the whole of Romans.[52] Thirdly, references are made to other parts of the corpus paulinum.[53] Nygren further holds that the idea of the two aeons is in fact the idea Paul intended to put forward. The interpretation is

---

[47] Barth 1926 pp 201f, 487–489.

[48] Cf the analysis in chapter four of the following issues: the identity of ἐγώ, the relation between the two covenants, how Jesus Christ brought salvation to human beings, the character of Christ-ian life and the key to the interpretation of the theme of Romans.

[49] pp 98–100.

[50] Ibid on the historical argument.

[51] Nygren 1944 pp 26f, 1952 pp 19f.

[52] Nygren 1944 pp 24f, 1952 pp 17f.

[53] Nygren 1944 pp 29f, 1952 pp 22f.

thus also supported by an intentional argument.[54] Thus, Nygren claims that the idea of the two aeons is based on reconstructive arguments of three kinds: contextual, historical and intentional, implying that his creative purpose is subordinated to his critical purposes. Are these claims justified? There are constructive arguments that point the other way.

Nygren asserts that secularization has made it difficult for many people to understand the idea of the two aeons, while "Christianity's own view of itself" includes it.[55] Furthermore, "For the men of the Reformation this understanding of the gospel and the consciousness of the two aeons were both living facts."[56] These two statements convey first a central idea of Nygren's well-known motif research. This idea implies that the view which emerges as a result of a motif analysis is correct.[57] Thus Nygren claims not only to put forward an interpretation of Romans, but claims to make the interpretation of Romans which is correct. Secondly, Nygren's dependence on the Reformers' theological distinction between the law and the gospel is evident. Nygren draws heavily on the Lutheran tradition and includes the distinction between the law and the gospel as an argument for his interpretation of Romans. The argument must be classified as constructive, since the assumption is far too developed to be classified as a reconstructive argument.[58] These two circumstances weaken Nygren's claims that his constructive interpretations are based on reconstructive interpretations. Furthermore, this idea is put forward as early as the introduction to Nygren's commentary and thus constitutes a clear point of departure.[59]

Does Nygren do what he claims to be doing? Yes he does – in the sense that he states clearly already in the introduction that he is going to interpret Paul in terms of the idea of the two aeons. No, he does not – in the sense that the reconstructive arguments do not provide a sufficient basis for the ontological, theological and anthropological idea of the two aeons. We have seen that the idea is far too well-developed to be classified other than as an anthropological, ontological and theological assumption and that Nygren claims to give the correct interpretation of Romans, which belongs to a creative purpose. Nygren's critical purpose does not take him as far as he claims. Rather, Nygren's creative purpose is given priority. The content of the constructive assumptions is however clearly expressed. Although Nygren does not admit its

---

[54] Nygren 1944 pp 28–30, 1952 pp 20–23.
[55] Nygren 1944 p 32, 1952 p 25.
[56] Ibid.
[57] Nygren 1930 pp 12–17, 1953 pp 34–40.
[58] Nygren 1944 pp 52f, 1952 pp 45f. Cf also Wingren's criticism of the fact that Nygren does not stick to his own programme by using Luther as a point of orientation and by not understanding the law as the Old Testament law, Wingren 1958 pp 91 and 99f.
[59] Nygren 1944 pp 23–33, 1952 pp 16–26.

constructive character, he does not deny the importance given to it for his creative purpose.

Wilckens pursues several critical purposes in order to obtain the limited creative purpose of recalling the Protestant and Catholic churches to theological unity. Priority is given in his commentary to the critical purposes. In terms of reconstructive and constructive interpretations Wilckens should pursue reconstructive interpretations to solve the ecumenical problem and his constructive arguments should thus be restricted to the assumption that the theological unity of the church ought to be promoted.

However, the analysis in chapter four showed that the contents of Wilckens' constructive arguments are not restricted to that assumption.[60] As in Barth's, Nygren's and Cranfield's commentaries, the contents of Wilckens' constructive arguments can be summarized as relating to some recurrent points of view, although they do not constitute an interpretive basis in the same sense as in the commentaries of the others. Wilckens holds the Christian to be changed decisively, so as both to know and do the will of God; he takes a positive view of Judaism in relation to Christianity and he holds the essence of the gospel to be about unity.

Wilckens' commentary however differs from the others' in that it also gives a comprehensive analysis of the historical context of Romans, which constitutes a reconstructive interpretive basis in his commentary. The content of the historical arguments is clear: Wilckens asserts that there is a decisive difference between Greek and Jewish thinking and that this finds expression in his account of the "Tun-Ergehen-Zusammenhang". Wilckens further refers to the situation of the Roman congregation, which is shaped by the discussion with the synagogue, for example, and the situation of the church, which is characterized by a threatened split.[61]

First, we will examine whether Wilckens actually fulfils his creative goal of recalling the church to theological unity on the basis of reconstructive interpretations. Secondly, we shall examine more carefully the role of his constructive arguments.

Wilckens has examples of reconstructive interpretations which support his creative purpose. The connection between the critical and the creative purposes is clear in respect of the interpretation of the way in which Christ brought salvation to mankind. The reconstructive interpretation is supported by arguments containing the idea of the "Tun-Ergehen-Zusammenhang" and its development,[62] contextual support for the cultic origin of this complex of

[60] See e g chapter four on the identity of ἐγώ, what characterizes Christian life and Paul's Jewish origin.
[61] Cf chapter four, all issues except the significance of Paul's Jewish origin, but this is because that analysis was limited to a single kind of argument.
[62] Cf pp 85–87. See also Wilckens 1978 (1) pp 130 (excursus) and 236–239 (excursus).

ideas[63] and the idea of Paul's new dialectical thought.[64] The theological viewpoint examined is the Catholic-Protestant disagreement about whether the atonement is to be understood as something which is merely given to the sinner (imputed) or as something which changes his or her whole character. Against the Catholic-Protestant disagreement Wilckens holds that both traditions ought to go back to the biblical view, which teaches that reconciliation is not just God's gift, but also God's saving power (that is, Wilckens argues against the Protestant theory of imputation in my interpretation).[65] Wilckens thus finds the basis for the solution of the Catholic-Protestant disagreement in his reconstructive arguments and on this issue keeps the critical and creative purposes firmly apart.

Some general problems nevertheless exist concerning the connection between these two kinds of purposes. First, in what way can ancient texts provide solutions to present-day problems? In this case, Romans even formed a basis for Luther's conflict with the Catholic church. The meaning of theological concepts has become very complex over the centuries. They are related not only to the biblical texts, but also to the view of the church, for example. The problem then becomes twofold: the original meaning is obscured by our theologically developed expressions and the original meaning of these expressions does not meet the theologically developed ideas. Wilckens risks anachronism, ignoring this difficult problem of the conditions behind the relation between his two kinds of purposes. Secondly, a question is raised in this connection by the implied claims of historical-critical exegesis: can biblical exegesis really be expected to solve ecumenical theological problems? Wilckens is very optimistic about this.[66] Is it right to see some opinions as pure misunderstandings as in the case of imputation? Is it likely that contradictory theological standpoints are only misinterpretations of one and the same idea? This is not clear, and Wilckens develops no theory concerning the connection between biblical exegesis and systematic theology.

Let us finally, however, examine whether Wilckens succeeds in something that is more complex than he actually intended. A plausible explanation of the presence of constructive arguments without reference to the idea that the theological union of the church ought to be promoted is that Wilckens is seeking to achieve his limited constructive purpose by referring to both reconstructive and constructive interpretations. Let us therefore examine whether

[63] Wilckens 1978 (1) pp 193f.
[64] Wilckens 1978 (1) p 279.
[65] Wilckens 1978 (1) p 201 (Zusammenfassung): "Denn dem theologischen Bewußtsein der Moderne ist der biblische Sühnegedanke als Horizont der Rechtfertigung weitgehend verlorengegangen. Ihn redlich und überzeugend neu zu gewinnen ist eine entscheidende gemeinsame Aufgabe der Theologie beider Konfessionen." See also p 202 (Zusammmenfassung).
[66] Wilckens 1978 (1) p vi.

Wilckens also has a wider creative purpose and sets out actually to solve the ecumenical problem by a combination of reconstructive and constructive interpretations.[67] Wilckens' interpretation of the key to the understanding of the theme of Romans provides an example of this.

Wilckens believes that the key to the interpretation of the theme of Romans lies in the idea that the gospel is all-embracing. This view is supported by contextual, historical and constructive arguments. I have already pointed to the complex relationship between this view and the arguments which support it.[68] It is difficult to decide which argument is the basis for which. Leaving that problem aside, let us see how the historical and constructive arguments are interrelated with the limited creative purpose of resolving the ecumenical division on this issue. Do the reconstructive and constructive interpretations together lead to a solution of the different Catholic and Protestant understandings of Christianity?

Wilckens believes that the key to the interpretation of the theme of Romans concerns an interplay between historical fact and the essence of the gospel. The historical situation is characterized by the threatened division of the church. Wilckens further describes the role of the Jerusalem collection in this situation. The collection is of political importance. It will contribute to the unity of the church as well as to the unity between Jews and Gentiles.[69] The essence of the gospel concerns the unity of all, Jews and Gentiles, Jewish and Gentile Christians.[70] This is the content of the reconstructive (historical) and constructive arguments. Wilckens assumes a similarity between the threatened split in the church at the time of Paul and the division in the church in our own generation and believes that the essence of Paul's gospel implies a call for unity also today.[71]

Let us first examine the connection between the historical and the constructive arguments. Wilckens observes that there is a difference between the gospel's being about unity and unity concerning this understanding of the essence of the gospel. Wilckens asserts that Paul was eager to reject his oppo-

---

[67] Wilckens 1978 (1) pp 51f points to some extent in that direction. Wilckens refers to Barth's, Bultmann's, Käsemann's, Cerfaux', Lyonnet's and Kuss' commentaries as combinations of historical-critical and " 'kerygmatisch'-religiöse Exegese" as a way of meeting the needs of the church and of Christianity.

[68] Cf p 98.

[69] Wilckens 1978 (1) pp 44–46 and 1982 (3) pp 128–131 (130–131 Zusammenfassung), especially 1978 (1) p 45: The collection "sollte zu einem unübersehbaren Erweis jener Einheit von Juden und Heiden unter dem Evangelium werden . . ."

[70] Wilckens 1978 (1) p 85.

[71] Wilckens 1978 (1) pp vi, 51f and 73 (Zusammenfassung).

nents opposite understanding of the gospel.[72] The collection was intended to express a unity despite these differences on the understanding of the essence of the gospel. The collection also however in this way expressed Paul's understanding of the gospel, the unity of all.[73] Thus, despite the fact that the collection does not express unity concerning Paul's and his opponents' understanding of the gospel – the opponents still entertain their own opinions – it expresses Paul's gospel of unity.[74]

The crucial point is how this combination of reconstructive and constructive interpretations is related to Wilckens' purpose of overcoming the theological conflict between the Protestant and Catholic churches. Basing himself on the similarity between the historical situation of the church at the time of Paul and at the present time, Wilckens holds that the message of Paul's epistle to the divided church of today is a call to unity, a unity which implies overcoming traditional theological conflicts. However, in Wilckens' interpretation of Romans, this does not correspond to the connection between the historical situation of Romans and Paul's understanding of the essence of the gospel. The theme of Romans is not unity on the understanding of the gospel, but that the gospel is about unity. A (historical) act of loyalty, the collection, is pursued by Paul despite points of disagreement concerning the understanding of the gospel.

Thus, the connection between the reconstructive and constructive arguments, on the one hand, and the limited creative purpose of calling the church to theological unity, on the other, does not hold good. Wilckens has not observed the consequences for his creative purpose of the difference between Paul's understanding that the gospel is about unity and unity concerning this understanding of the essence of the gospel. However good the cause of recalling the Protestant and Catholic churches to unity in their understanding of the gospel, Wilckens has not succeeded in establishing a basis for this by his reconstructive and constructive interpretations of Romans. Rather, his interpretation implies that what the Protestant and Catholic churches should do is not seek unity in the content of faith, i e the essence of the gospel, but express their unity in acts of loyalty, corresponding to the Jerusalem collection. In calling the church to unity, Wilckens thus moves away from the connection between his critical and creative purposes and is purely creative.

---

[72] Wilckens 1978 (1) p 45 and 1980 (2) p 209 (Zusammenfassung): "Nicht eine allgemeine Lehre von der Willensfreiheit Gottes, die sich in doppelter Prädestination verwirklicht, will Paulus entfalten, sondern der Empörung des jüdischen Partners gegen das Erwählungshandeln Gottes in der christlichen Gegenwart, gegen die Kirche aus Juden und Heiden, mit deren Berufung die Exklusivität Israels als alleiniges Gottesvolk aufgehoben sei, will er den Mund stopfen."

[73] Wilckens 1978 (1) p 45.

[74] Wilckens 1978 (1) pp 69f (Zusammenfassung) and 1982 (3) pp 129–131. However, Wilckens 1978 (1) p 70 (Zusammenfassung) shows he is aware of the problem implied in this idea.

We can conclude that Wilckens does not use only reconstructive arguments for the creative purpose of ending the divisions in the church. He refers also to constructive arguments, primarily an interpretation of the essence of the gospel, which make the relation between his critical and creative purposes more complex than he has indicated.

Still, Wilckens also at times leaves the constructive arguments aside and argues only with reconstructive arguments as a basis for his creative purpose as concerning how Jesus Christ brought salvation to human beings. However, the connection between Wilckens' two kinds of purposes involves some problems that he does not discuss. Wilckens does not examine the relation between the old text and the modern questions, nor does he develop a theory concerning the relation between biblical exegesis and systematic theology, although implying that biblical exegesis bears directly on systematic theology.

Finally, the basis for the connection between the critical purposes, the constructive arguments and the creative purpose of calling the divided church to theological unity, proves weak. This is due to the failure to distinguish between the idea that the gospel is about unity and unity concerning this understanding of the gospel when the interpretation of Romans is related to the situation of today.

3. Conclusions

First, we can conclude that Barth's, Nygren's, Cranfield's and Wilckens' commentaries explicitly pursue a combination of purposes.

Secondly, we can conclude that Barth, Nygren and Wilckens explicitly combine purposes of two different types: critical and creative purposes. These are combined in different ways. Barth gives priority to the creative purpose, while Wilckens gives priority to the critical purpose. Nygren intends to give priority to the critical purpose, but it is evident that the results of his critical analysis come closer to Barth's creative results than to Cranfield's and Wilckens' critical results. Cranfield has only critical purposes.

Thirdly, if the commentators' prime purposes are taken into account some explanations can be given concerning their different interpretations and general remarks. We can also conclude that critical commentaries can deal with theological themes. Furthermore, creative commentaries can deal with the original meaning of the text, since a commentary may have both critical and creative purposes.

However, Nygren's and Wilckens' commentaries reveal a complicated relation between the two types of purposes. This was further examined in the second section of this chapter. The basic problem to be answered was: do the commentators achieve their aims? In order to answer that question the critical and creative purposes were related to the reconstructive and constructive interpretations from chapter four. From this analysis it was possible to conclude, fourthly, that the results of the commentaries differ from their purposes except in the case of Barth's commentary. Let me develop this a little.

Barth fulfils his purposes and is aware of the epistemological weakness in his commentary. Nygren fulfils his purposes in the sense that the content of the idea of the two aeons decides his interpretations and general remarks. However, I cannot agree with Nygren's characterization of his purposes. Nygren's commentary is less critical than he admits. The greatest discrepancy is to be found in Cranfield's commentary. It is by no means purely critical, as the author tells his readers. Wilckens' commentary fulfils his purposes from time to time. But Wilckens does not discuss the problems implied in the relation between his critical and creative purposes concerning the connections between ancient texts and modern problems, and between biblical exegesis and systematic theology. Furthermore, his own use of constructive arguments complicates the relation between his purposes in a way not observed by himself. Finally, if Wilckens is taken to pursue a combination of reconstructive and constructive arguments for his limited creative purpose, we must conclude that this undertaking also fails, since Wilckens does not acknowledge the difference between Paul's gospel of unity and unity concerning Paul's gospel.

If the actual relations between the purposes of the commentaries are taken into account, we find that the creative purpose receives priority in the commentaries of both Barth and Nygren. This is not explicitly stated in Nygren's commentary, since Nygren insists that his critical purposes take him further than they actually do. Thus, Nygren's explicit purpose is slightly misleading. However, the problem of where the border lies between Nygren's critical and creative purposes is obvious to the reader in one respect, since Nygren's critical claims are clearly stated in the introduction. In Cranfield's commentary the relation between the critical and creative purposes is implicit, since his creative purpose is explicitly denied. This misleads the reader and blurs the connection between Cranfield's reconstructive and constructive interpretations. When analysed, however, the implicit critical and creative purposes are quite clearly connected. The contents of the constructive arguments constitute the interpretive basis which the reconstructive arguments supplement. Finally, the explicit relation between the critical and creative purposes in Wilckens' commentary is blurred. This is due to the presence of constructive arguments which do not refer to the theological unity of the church and to Wilckens' failure to draw the proper conclusions from his critical analysis.

My use of the expressions explict and implicit purposes above does not imply that an implicit purpose is not clearly present, but that it is not explicitly stated as a purpose of the commentary. The discrepancy between what the commentators say they are doing and what they actually do is clear from the reading of the commentaries. It is no part of this study to explain this fact. However, it seems to me that the answer may be sought in the fixed form of the genre. Explicit penetration of the purposes of the commentaries is absent from these and most other commentaries. The literary conventions of commentary-writing obviously allow for mistakes that are unsatisfactory. It is possible to hold that a commentary may have both critical and creative purposes; but the commentators' failure to keep them apart, sometimes even denying one purpose, misleads the reader. Biblical commentaries would benefit from serious treatment of this issue.

The explicit purposes of the commentaries offer some explanation of the differences between them. However, the principal result of this analysis has been that the results achieved by the commentators differ from their explicit purposes in varying degrees, except in the case of Barth. In a sense this might also be considered an explanation of the differences. The fundamentally indistinct nature of Nygren's, Cranfield's and Wilckens' commentaries in respect of their purposes does nothing to improve their chances of arriving at similar interpretations or general remarks.

Chapter Six

Some Basic Assumptions of the Commentaries

In this chapter I examine whether Barth's, Nygren's, Cranfield's and Wilckens' different interpretations of Romans 7, some theological themes of Romans and their different general remarks on Romans can be explained by reference to the authors' views of the content of Christian faith and of some more basic theological assumptions: their views of revelation and the Bible, and the problem of application.

Barth's, Nygren's, Cranfield's and Wilckens' views of the content of Christian faith are set out in the first section. The section consists in the main of summaries of the content of their constructive arguments. I have refrained from giving cross-references, because I believe these summaries will be familiar to the reader. In other respects I refer generally to chapter four.

Some of the differences concerning the content of Christian faith raise basic theological problems. However, since these issues are more or less implicit in the commentaries, these analyses are more tentative than those in chapters four and five. I have refrained from seeking support in other works by the commentators. This may appear a divergence from the reasonable interpretation aimed at in this study. But commentaries on the Bible must be regarded as independent works, which it is every bit as justified to compare with other commentaries as it is to compare them with the rest of the authors' productions. Furthermore, the purpose of this thesis is to analyse the internal dynamics of the commentaries. Therefore I examine the ways in which the differences between the commentaries may be explained by reference to the views of revelation and the Bible which the commentaries indicate. Finally, I raise a problem actualized by the whole of part two, i e the problem of application. In the conclusion I ask which commentary offers the best interpretation and make a suggestion about how future commentaries on Romans might be improved.

1. The content of Christian faith

In part one we saw that Barth's, Nygren's, Cranfield's and Wilckens' interpretations of Romans 7 and some theological themes as well as their general remarks on Romans differ considerably. One explanation was found in chapter four, where the decisive character of the constructive arguments was observed. Consequently, a possible explanation for the differences between the commentaries may be that they differ in the constructive assumptions they make, i e concerning their anthropological, ontological, philosophical and theological arguments. In this section I will first recapitulate some differences in content of the constructive arguments used by Barth, Nygren, Cranfield and Wilckens. Secondly, I will draw attention to some less explicit differences which also concern the content of Christian faith.

One decisive difference between Barth's, Nygren's, Cranfield's and Wilckens' anthropological arguments is that on a scale from pessimistic to optimistic anthropology Barth is the most pessimistic, and also sees Christian life on this earth in sharp contrast to God's will and purpose. Nygren comes second, since he holds Christian life to be characterized by both the old and the new aeons. Wilckens is third, with a more optimistic view of what the Christian is capable of, and Cranfield is the most optimistic, understanding the Christian to be capable of obedience to God. A second difference between the anthropologies of the commentaries is that Cranfield and Wilckens describe human beings very much in moral terms, while Barth and Nygren do not.

Another difference is that both Barth and Nygren draw on a dualistic ontology, and Cranfield and Wilckens do not. In Barth's commentary the dualism is related to an assumption of dialectical philosophy. Wilckens also draws on dialectical philosophy, but without making the ontological connection. Also, while Barth focuses on the antitheses, Wilckens focuses on the syntheses.

Another difference concerns the image of God. Cranfield refers most to his image of God as loving and severe in constructive arguments. In chapter two, it was possible to see that Wilckens shares this view, while Barth and Nygren stress God's love at the expense of his severity.

Another basic difference can be discerned, for example, in the commentators' different interpretations of the relation between the covenants. Cranfield and Wilckens hold that there is a harmonious relation and a continuity between the covenants, while Barth and Nygren stress the contrast between them. As a consequence, Barth and Nygren do not value the law as high as Cranfield and Wilckens. Barth and Nygren also see Paul's Christian life in opposition to his Jewish background, while Cranfield and Wilckens understand Paul's Jewish background to be in harmony with his Christian identity.

These differences point to a difference concerning the apprehension of the unique nature of Christianity. Barth and Nygren hold that Christianity must be seen in sharp contrast to Judaism, while Cranfield and Wilckens hold that Christianity must be seen against the Old Testament background and hold that there is a continuity between the two religions.[1]

A more careful look at the anthropologies of the commentators reveals differences concerning the moral aspect of sin and concerning the radical nature of human sin. According to Cranfield and Wilckens, sin is basically concerned with the transgression of the law, i e morals, while according to Barth and Nygren, sin concerns the whole man. Cranfield and Wilckens furthermore understand Christian life to be something radically new, since it is possible to lead a new life through moral improvement, while Barth and Nygren are more pessimistic about the moral renewal of the Christians.

These differences point to a difference concerning the understanding of evil. It is possible to make a distinction between moral and non-moral evil.[2] Moral evil is evil caused by the will of Man, while non-moral evil is something that occurs independent of human will, e g floods and earthquakes. In the commentaries evil is primarily related to sin. Moral sin is disobedience to the will of God, while non-moral sin is rather the tragic human predicament, not restricted to morals, but including what just happens to human beings independent of their own actions. Either kind of sin can furthermore be apprehended as more or less radical. A less radical view of evil holds human sin to be open to correction, while a more radical view holds that sin is not open to correction.

It follows from the differences we observed concerning the commentators' Christian anthropologies that Barth and Nygren have a radical and primarily non-moral understanding of evil, while Cranfield and Wilckens have a less radical and primarily moral understanding of evil.

Thus, Barth's, Nygren's, Cranfield's and Wilckens' different interpretations of Romans 7 and some theological themes, and their different general remarks on Romans may be partly explained by reference to their different views of the content of Christian faith. These differences are not confined to explicit arguments; they may be observed in their interpretations of Romans, as in the case of the image of God.

To explain these differences goes beyond the limits of this thesis. However, it is obvious that two factors are important: the theological traditions of the commentators, including their denomination and their academic milieu at different universities, and their cultural situation in a wider sense. These commentators' different views of the unique nature of Christianity have with-

---

[1] See Barth 1926 pp 316f, where Israel is identified as the church and said to be in opposition to the gospel, Nygren 1944 pp 113f, 1952 p 108, where Nygren regrets that people have lost the concept of "heathendom" and concludes "In it he (Paul) saw no divine revelation at all", Cranfield 1986 (2) pp 446 and 828 (essays) on the close connection to the Old Testament and Wilckens 1980 (2) p 185, where he holds that the church has by and large viewed Judaism in contrast to Christianity, which is not in accordance with Paul's view.

[2] Hick 1973 p 38.

out a doubt been affected by the horrors of the holocaust.[3] The cultural situation alters the terms of theological discussions.

2. The views of revelation

Barth's and Nygren's dualistic ontologies and emphasis on the way in which God is totally unlike anything that is human, the commentators' different understandings of the relation between the covenants – as contrary or harmonious – and their different views of the unique nature of Christianity point to another explanation, namely different views of revelation.

The differences in their views of revelation concern a new theological level compared with the differences concerning the content of Christian faith. Questions concerning revelation belong to the prolegomena of systematic theology or to the philosophy of religion. Logically it is a more fundamental issue. I will examine whether the differences referred to above can also be explained as differences in the view of revelation.

The basic question about revelation is: how do human beings attain a knowledge of God? This question contains also the question of how revelation is to be related to natural human knowledge.

There are at least three ways of relating revelation to natural human knowledge. First, one can hold that there is no natural knowledge of God. All knowledge of God comes through revelation. This is a *revelation positivist view*. Secondly, one can hold that natural human knowledge is sufficient for attaining a knowledge of God. This is a *rationalistic view*. Thirdly, one can hold that it is possible to attain some knowledge of God by natural human knowledge, but that it is complemented, in one way or another, by what God reveals of himself, i e a *connection-theory*.[4]

Barth's commentary points in the direction of a revelation positivist view.[5] The abyss that separates God and man is very wide. Further, all other religions are mistaken and contrary to Christianity. Man knows nothing of God except through the revelation in Christ.[6] Nygren's commentary points the

---

[3] See Wilckens 1980 (2) pp 267f (Zusammenfassung).

[4] Cf Holte 1984 p 83.

[5] This might seem like a trivial characterization, since Barth is the typos of a revelation positivist. However, *Der Römerbrief* belongs to Barth's earlier production and the dualistic ontology was not as developed in the first edition of his commentary. God is not depicted there as totally different and he does act in this world. See Barth 1919 p 14: "Denn Gott kann *geschaut* werden". See also p 254: "Diese neue Gewalt über die Dinge ist die Gewalt Gottes", indicating a closer relation between God and this world. See also pp 121–124, cf Barth 1926 pp 223f and 341f.

[6] E g Barth 1926 p 62: People who claim they have experience of God are held to be wrong. True faith is emptiness, "Hohlraum". See also p 270: "Der Geist ist die Wahrheit."

same way, although his position is less inclusive than Barth's. God's love is unfathomable and the revelation in Christ is opposed to every other religion, which is "heathendom".[7]

Cranfield and Wilckens do not stress God's quality of being *totaliter aliter*, nor do they share Barth's and Nygren's dualistic ontology. Rather, they stress the continuity between the covenants. Cranfield's and Wilckens' commentaries both point in the direction of other views of revelation.

Cranfield's commentary however also shows some similarities with those of Barth and Nygren. Cranfield holds that human beings can neither know God, nor know how to lead a moral life except through faith in the revelation of God.[8] Thus, Cranfield basically takes a revelation positivist view, which differs from Barth's and Nygren's in being less Christocentric.

Wilckens' commentary points in a different direction altogether. He explicitly holds a connection-theory. Wilckens holds that there is no conflict between the knowledge attained by human reasoning and the knowledge attained through revelation.[9]

Thus, the differences between the commentators can partly be explained by their holding different views of revelation.

Another aspect of the view of revelation also seems to play a part. If the issue of the theme of Romans is taken together with the commentators' different attitudes toward the importance of knowledge of the Roman situation for the proper understanding of the Epistle, a pattern can be discerned. Barth does not hold knowledge of the historical situation of Romans to be decisive for the interpretation of Romans. He develops its theme by reference to the idea of the double predestination. Nygren does not take knowledge of the historical situation of Romans to be decisive for the interpretation of Romans either. When developing the theme he refers to a hidden pattern, special to Paul: the idea of the two aeons. Cranfield takes historical knowledge to be important and develops the theme of Romans with the aid of the Old Testament background. Finally, Wilckens also takes historical knowledge to be important and develops the theme of Romans with reference to the gospel of unity, which he believes is closely connected with the historical situation of the church at the time of Paul.

---

[7] Nygren 1944 pp 113f, 1952 p 108. Nygren's close relation between the critical and creative purposes could be taken as evidence of a more rationalistic view of revelation. However, I have rather understood Nygren's revelation positivist view as compatible with human reasoning.

[8] Cranfield 1985 (1) pp 116 and 410. On morals see 1986 (2) pp 595, 609f and 646. See also p 604f on 12:1: "For Paul the true worship is rational not in the sense of being consistent with the natural rationality of man (. . .), but in the sense of being consistent with a proper understanding of the truth of God revealed in Jesus Christ."

[9] Wilckens 1980 (2) pp 140–145 (Zusammenfassung) on 8:1–17. Cf 1978 (1) pp 116–121 (Zusammenfassung) on 1:1–32, where Wilckens compares the views of Thomas Aquinas and Barth and concludes that they are both compatible with his form of connection-theory.

I shall now examine whether these differences can be explained by reference to another aspect of revelation, namely the commentators' understanding of where revelation takes place in relation to the Bible.

It is generally possible to differentiate between a propositional and a nonpropositional view of revelation related to the text of the Bible. According to a propositional view, revelation is essentially found in the text. According to a non-propositional view, revelation is not in the text, and the text is seen rather as a witness to revelation, which is often held to take place in events in history. We will however need a more subtle instrument to enable us to clarify the differences between Barth's, Nygren's, Cranfield's and Wilckens' commentaries. I shall differentiate between two kinds of clearly non-propositional views and two less clearly non-propositional views, one of which comes close to a propositional view.

First, it is possible to hold that revelation takes place when God reveals himself in historical events. Revelation is readily apprehended by at least some people and the Bible is the record of these events. Secondly, one can hold that God's revelation takes place instead on an existential level. The events recorded in the Bible, for example, are not themselves mediators of revelation. Rather, revelation is something which takes place by an interaction of God and the human mind, e g when biblical texts are recited or preached upon. I call the first a *historical* non-propositional view of revelation and the second an *existential* non-propositional view of revelation.[10] These two views both focus on non-verbal revelation.

On the other hand, at least two different ways exist of focusing instead on the verbal interpretation of revelation.[11] The first relates indirectly to what is understood as God's revelation, while the second ties God's revelation closer to the verbal interpretation itself and thus comes closest to a propositional view of revelation. The first view implies that although God has revealed himself non-verbally in history, this revelation is only accessible to people through the human interpretation of revelation, which is found also in the Bible. A common word for these human verbal interpretations of revelation is tradition. I call this view an *indirect traditional* non-propositional view of revelation. However, some hold that instead of being localised in non-verbal history revelation should be localised precisely in its verbal interpretation. God's revelation is found in tradition as we find it in the Bible. I call this a

[10] This distinction has been inspired by Hick and Jeffner. Hick identifies the non-propositional view as "the *heilsgeschichtlich* view", Hick 1973 p 59. Jeffner points out that, according to some theologians, there is a kind of existential religious experience which itself is part of revelation, Jeffner 1981 pp 73–77.

[11] The following two categories have been inspired by Barr's arguing that the divine inspiration should be understood in terms of God's presence among his people "in the formation of their tradition and in the crystallization of that tradition as a scripture . . .", Barr 1983 p 18.

direct traditional non-propositional view of revelation. It is a matter of degree how close the connection between tradition and God's revelation is understood to be, and this depends on different views of the accessibility of God's revelation. Some would hold the human part in tradition to be significant, while others, coming close to the propositional view, would hold it to be less so.

Although Barth, Nygren, Cranfield and Wilckens understand the Bible to be God's word (see the next section), they do not hold it to be identical with God's word and thus do not subscribe to a propositional view of the Bible. Writing a biblical commentary with some degree of critical distance to the biblical text implies some kind of non-propositional view.

In Barth's commentary we can find explicit statements which place him at the existential non-propositional end of the scale. Paul is only bearing witness to revelation in Romans. It concentrates on Christ, not on the historical Jesus, and the theological significance of historical events does not belong to these events themselves; revelation is something that takes place on an existential level.[12]

The way in which Nygren ties the theme of Romans so closely to Paul's own expression points to a view at the other end of the scale. The thoughts of Paul are true expressions of the gospel. Nygren's non-propositional view of revelation can thus be classified as a direct traditional view. I judge that Nygren regards the human part in tradition to be quite small. However, Nygren apparently does not evaluate everything in this tradition as equally important.[13]

Thus, although Barth and Nygren share a revelation positivist view, they differ considerably in their non-propositional views. This may explain the difference in their development of the theme of Romans. Neither refers to the historical circumstances. But while Nygren holds his understanding to be in accordance with Paul's own text, Barth is free to use the anachronistic theological term of the double predestination.

Both Cranfield and Wilckens stress the importance of historical knowledge for the proper understanding of Romans. Does this mean that their commentaries point in the direction of a historical non-propositional view of revelation? In Wilckens' case the answer is Yes. This becomes very clear when his critical and creative purposes are related to each other. Wilckens localises the interpretive basis in the historical circumstances. Wilckens also states explicitly that the mysteries of God are revealed in the "Geschichte".[14] However, the historical arguments in Cranfield's commentary are few. Instead, he

---

[12] Barth 1926 p 511, where Barth states that Christ is not contained in any book, pp 5f on Jesus only being meaningful as Christ, cf p 123f, further on the existentiality of faith, p 366, cf p 298.

[13] Nygren 1944 p 26, 1952 p 19, where Nygren wants Paul to interpret himself. For Nygren not evaluating everything as equally important see the thematic way in which he writes and the brief notes on Romans 14–16.

[14] Wilckens 1978 (1) pp 86f.

stresses the importance of the Old Testament. Cranfield also stresses that in order to obtain "anything approaching an objective understanding" of Romans it is necessary to stay close to the text.[15] Cranfield nevertheless distinguishes between the word of God and the Bible.[16] Thus, Cranfield's commentary points in the direction of an indirect traditional non-propositional view in that he differs both from Nygren's direct traditional and Wilckens' historical views. This makes Cranfield's and Nygren's commentaries alike in stressing tradition. Possibly this constitutes the common basis for their evaluation of Romans as the best expression of the gospel.[17]

Thus, the differences between the commentaries cannot be explained merely by the fact that they point in different directions concerning the epistemological aspect of revelation, but also by the fact that they point in different directions concerning the question of where revelation is localised, i e their different non-propositional views.

3. The views of the Bible

It is already clear from the different views the commentators take of revelation that Barth, Nygren, Cranfield and Wilckens differ concerning their views of the Bible. This will be developed a little further in this section.

In chapter four we saw that Barth, Nygren, Cranfield and Wilckens all refer to constructive arguments. When related to their purposes, we found that these arguments played different roles in the commentaries. In Barth's commentary they are self-evident in relation to his prime creative purpose of expressing Christian faith today. They are also frequent. In Nygren's commentary they are motivated by the close connection between his critical and creative purposes. However, in Cranfield's and Wilckens' commentaries the constructive arguments are puzzling. The importance of their constructive arguments does not accord with their prime critical purposes.

I want now to examine whether this similarity[18] in the use of constructive arguments can be explained by reference to the circumstance that they hold in some ways similar views of the Bible. For the sake of clarity, I propose here also to refer to some distinctions that I will not need later on.

The basic question about the Bible is this: is the Bible the word of God? If it is, in what sense is the Bible God's word? It should be noted that answering this question lies beyond the limits of the critical purpose. It is a creative deci-

---

[15] Cranfield 1986 (2) p 819 (essays). See also p 734: "All Scripture has its relevance and applicability to us . . ."

[16] Cranfield 1986 (2) p 818 n 2 (essays) and p 850 n 3 (essays).

[17] Cf p 63.

[18] In contrast to the other issues it is not a difference, but a similarity that needs explanation.

sion based on the author's belief or non-belief. If the answer to the first question is No, then the Bible is seen as an expression of the human phenomenon of religion. If the answer is Yes, the second question also has to be answered. Basically, two answers are possible: either God's word is identical with the words of the Bible – a *literal inspiration* view – or God's word is contained in or mediated through the words of the Bible. This latter view, like the view that the Bible is an expression of the human phenomenon of religion, is compatible with historical criticism. For this reason such views are often referred to as *historical-critical* views of the Bible. The literary inspiration view of the Bible is not compatible with historical-critical scholarship because it does not allow for the possibility that something stated in the Bible may be wrong, while the critical study of the Bible does not rule this out.[19]

Defining historical-critical scholarship is no easy task. The concept covers many different variations.[20] That aside, we can say that historical-critical biblical scholarship implies that critical methods of different kinds, although generally historical in some sense, are justified when studying the Bible.

In order to explain the differences between Barth's, Nygren's, Cranfield's and Wilckens' commentaries, however, we need to make yet another distinction concerning whether the interpreters hold the Bible to be the word of God or not. Strictly speaking, this distinction is not part of the view of the Bible. Instead, we might say that the different views of the Bible imply different attitudes towards historical criticism.

If the Bible is held not to be God's word, the scholar has a *secular* attitude to historical-critical scholarship. If the Bible is held to be God's word, there are two possibilities. First, the scholar may accept that it is legitimate to use ordinary critical methods to study the Bible, but hold them inadequate to attain a proper understanding of it. These methods therefore need to be supplemented with methods which belong to the sphere of faith. The implication is that only the believer can interpret the Bible correctly. This I call a *transcendent* attitude to historical-critical scholarship. Secondly, the scholar may hold that, although the critical methods are insufficient to attain knowledge of the word of God aspect of the Bible, they are nevertheless justified, and the academic study of the Bible should be restricted to these methods on methodological grounds. This is generally justified on the grounds that a critical study of the Bible is a prerequisite for all biblical interpretation. The implication is that even a non-believer can perform biblical studies on equal terms. This I call a *methodological* attitude to historical-critical scholarship.

[19] Cf Barr 1981a pp 40 and 120–132.
[20] Cf Gunnlaugur 1988, who characterizes three different periods of Old Testament exegesis, and Morgan with Barton 1988 pp 44–166 for another historical review of different dominant features in biblical criticism.

Objections may be raised to the distinction between a secular and a methodological historical-critical attitude. However, as Morgan points out: "Since most biblical scholars have been religious as well as rational it is likely that much of their work has included an element of theological interpretation, no matter how honestly they have also plied their trade as historians and exegetes."[21] This distinction will prove useful when explaining the similarity between the use of constructive arguments in the commentaries.

Barth has a transcendent attitude to historical-critical scholarship. He is not opposed to historical criticism, but does not believe it is capable of bringing out the meaning of the text. "Aber nicht die historische Kritik mache ich ihnen zum Vorwurf, deren Recht und Notwendigkeit ich vielmehr noch einmal ausdrücklich anerkenne, sondern ihr Stehenbleiben bei einer Erklärung des Textes, die ich keine Erklärung nennen kann, sondern nur den ersten primitiven Versuch einer solchen, ..."[22]

Nygren's commentary is harder to classify. On the one hand he sets forth the reconstructive basis for his study, which is in harmony with his programme for motif research.[23] On the other hand, I have questioned the critical character of this understanding.[24] Thus, Nygren comes close to a transcendent attitude. Nygren's methodological approach does not rule out the assumption that the Bible is the word of God, but presupposes that by using his method, it is possible to arrive at a proper knowledge of the gospel, i e its religious content. With this reservation, I would classify Nygren's attitude as basically methodological. His claim to an objective basis is open to question, but he does not appear to believe that faith is a prerequisite of a proper understanding of Romans. I call Nygren's attitude modified methodological.

Barth's and Nygren's attitudes explain their frequent use of constructive arguments. According to Barth, these are necessary for a proper understanding of the Bible. According to Nygren, they have an objective basis.

Cranfield and Wilckens are clearly historical critics, who use the ordinary methods of criticism to comment on the text.[25] However, both also hold that the Bible is the word of God. According to Cranfield, "In the law, as everywhere else in the Bible, God's word is given to us through the words of men – with all that that involves"[26] and according to Wilckens the editor who added the concluding doxology "stellt so den Charakter der Theologie des Rö-

[21] Morgan with Barton 1988 p 274.
[22] Barth 1926 p x. See also p xii.
[23] Nygren 1944 p 17, 1952 p 9, where he refers to exegetical study and 1944 pp 94f, 1952 pp 86f, where he argues for the theme of Romans in meeting the argument "Are we guilty of subjectivity and an unrestrained impulse to systematize?" with "a purely objective statistical observation" of the frequency of some words.
[24] Cf pp 117–119.
[25] See the "General editors' preface", Cranfield 1985 (1) p vii and Wilckens 1978 (1) p v.
[26] Cranfield 1986 (2) p 850 n 3 (essays).

merbriefs als *Offenbarungs*theologie heraus."[27] Thus, they share a methodological, not a secular, attitude. Though their methodological approaches are not identical, the fact that they are not secular explains their use of constructive arguments to interpret Romans 7 and some theological themes, and to advance some general remarks on Romans.[28]

Thus, the similarity between Barth's, Nygren's, Cranfield's and Wilckens' commentaries in the use of constructive arguments can be explained by the similarity of their attitudes to the historical-critical approach to the Bible. Although different, they have one thing in common: they see the Bible, and Romans, as the word of God. The similarity can be explained by the fact that none of them has a secular attitude to the historical-critical study of the Bible.

4. The problem of application

Finally, one problem needs to be brought up which has been present right through part two. The analysis in chapter four showed the presence of both reconstructive and constructive arguments in the commentaries of Barth, Nygren, Cranfield and Wilckens. In chapter five these fundamental kinds of interpretations were related to the purposes of the commentaries. Although decisive for their interpretations of Romans, the constructive interpretations did not quite fit the aims given by Nygren, Cranfield and Wilckens. We have also seen in this chapter that basic theological assumptions play a part in the commentators' interpretation of Romans. Views concerning revelation as well as the commentators' understanding of the Bible as God's word are also constructive assumptions. Thus, as far as kinds of interpretations are concerned, the purposes of the commentaries and their views of revelation and the Bible all suggest that the problem of the relation between the reconstructive and constructive interpretations is of the utmost importance in these commentaries, not just in the sense that Barth, Nygren, Cranfield and Wilckens are relating reconstructive and constructive interpretations to each other, but more in the sense that the relation itself has proved problematic. The commentators do not seem sufficiently to observe the different characters of the interpretations. Barth apart, they do not do what they claim to be doing and they let their view of revelation influence their interpretation of Romans without clarifying their views to the reader.

It is often assumed that critical exegesis interprets the text up to a certain

[27] Wilckens 1982 (3) p 151 (Zusammenfassung), cf 1978 (1) pp vf.
[28] Wilckens differs from Cranfield in relating his historical-critical results to the theological development. They also differ concerning favoured scientific methods. While Wilckens stresses historical knowledge of the situation of Romans, Cranfield more often refers to philological arguments.

point; thereafter it is up to the systematic theologians to look to the application of the text.[29] However, the presence of constructive arguments in the commentaries of Barth, Nygren, Cranfield and Wilckens and their (implicit) creative purposes imply that the problem of application is present also in these commentaries.[30] In terms of reconstructive and constructive interpretations the problem of application is this: how should the shift be made from reconstructive to constructive interpretations of a text?

Some results taken from the earlier sections of part two give an idea of how Barth, Nygren, Cranfield and Wilckens solve the problem of application. Barth seems to hold the link between the reconstructive and constructive interpretations to be existential. Intuition and feelings of self-evidence are decisive.[31] Nygren appears to make this connection between the reconstructive and constructive interpretations using the idea of the two aeons, which is held to bear more or less directly on the constructive interpretation.[32] Cranfield avoids the question[33] and Wilckens regards the historical interpretations as decisive for his constructive interpretations.[34] Thus, in Nygren's and Wilckens' commentaries the problem of application is solved by reference to the close relation between the reconstructive and constructive interpretations. However, Barth's and Cranfield's commentaries make no such clear connection. Nygren's and Wilckens' solutions, furthermore, have a clear starting point in the reconstructive interpretations, while Barth's goes beyond the limits of the reconstructive interpretations and Cranfield intimates no solution at all to the problem.

Objections can be raised against all Barth's, Nygren's and Wilckens' solutions to the problem of application. The connection between Barth's existential knowledge and the content of the text of Romans verges on the arbitrary. Nygren's commentary also lacks a clear connection with the text; acceptance at any rate of the solution indicated by his commentary requires agreement both with his method and his analysis of the content of the theme in Romans. The solution indicated by Wilckens becomes unclear not in its connection with the text, but in its connection with the constructive inter-

---

[29] Cf Morgan with Barton 1988 p 16: "It is for theologians to decide how to use the Bible; biblical scholars simply say what it means. That at least is a commonly held view."

[30] Cf Jeffner 1981 pp 68–77 and 1982 pp 87–90.

[31] Barth 1926 pp 282f, 297 and 411. Cf above pp 115 f.

[32] Cf pp 108 f.

[33] Cranfield 1985 (1) p 1. One might ask, however, whether Cranfield's recurring argument of the moral relation between God and man does not constitute a link between historical-critical exegesis and creative theological application such as Nygren's idea of the two aeons. This is not the case. Cranfield develops no corresponding theory. Rather, the link between the argument of the moral relation and Cranfield's descriptive purposes has been shown to be very weak, see above p 114.

[34] Wilckens 1978 (1) pp vi and 52.

pretation. In the first place, it is difficult to understand exactly how the historical results bear on the theological conflicts between the Catholic and Protestant churches. Secondly, Wilckens fails to notice the need to consider the problem of applying the historical results to his own constructive assumptions. Thus, Barth's commentary has weaknesses concerning the reconstructive connection of the problem of application and Wilckens' has weaknesses concerning the constructive connection. The weakness of Nygren's commentary is that it centres too much on the connection itself and the weakness of Cranfield's commentary is that it lacks a clear connection.

Thus, the different solutions to the problem of application as well as the lack of such a solution may explain why the commentaries' interpretations of Romans differ so much. Barth's reference to intuition opens up an infinite variety of possible interpretations. This can be seen, for example, in his own different interpretations of Romans in the first two editions of his commentary. Nygren's reference to a specific constructive assumption also opens the way for new and various interpretations. Cranfield's failure to provide a solution to this problem contained in his commentary renders the various possibilities as arbitrary as does Barth's intuitive solution. Finally, Wilckens' solution to the problem of application opens the way for different interpretations, even should another interpreter share his reconstructive historical basis, since there is no clear connection between it and the constructive assumptions.

5. Conclusions

A proper conclusion to this last analysis would be to ask who is right. Which commentary gives the best interpretation of Romans?

In making up one's mind on such a difficult question, it is not necessary only to examine critically Barth's, Nygren's, Cranfield's and Wilckens' interpretations and general remarks as described in part one. When evaluating different points of view we generally examine the arguments put forward in their support. In part two I have formulated the kinds of interpretations as arguments capable of critical examination. The commentators' basic theological assumptions can also be regarded as arguments for their interpretations and general remarks.

In order to say which of these commentaries gives the best interpretation of Romans it is necessary to make up one's mind on a number of issues. The different philological, contextual, historical, intentional, natural, consistency and constructive arguments have to be examined. We have to decide who gives the best account of the content of Christian faith. We also have to make up our minds about their different views of revelation, including their different non-propositional views. Their different views of the Bible, or more to the point, their different attitudes towards historical-critical biblical scholarship also have to be evaluated. Finally, we must examine critically the different solutions they put forward to the problem of application. It should also be remembered that these issues are often interlinked to such a degree that to assess them one by one is impossible. This circumstance complicates the choice between the commentaries' interpretations, also concerning limited problems of interpretation.

It is not the purpose of this study to perform such a comprehensive evaluation. My contribution to the discussion of biblical interpretation lies in the fact that my detailed analysis of four contemporary commentaries on Paul's Epistle to the Romans has shown the puzzling and at the same time fascinating complexity of the interpretation process.

As to the puzzling aspect, the relation between reconstructive and constructive interpretations put forward in its different dimensions in chapters four, five and six, has been shown to give rise to recurring problems in the commentaries. One expression of this is that the problem of application is central and yet not satisfactorily resolved in these commentaries. I am convinced that a discussion of the problem of application would help resolve the problem of the different interpretations of the same text. First it would reveal the factors involved in the interpretation process: the different kinds of interpretations and purposes, the different views of the content of Christian faith and revelation, and certainly other factors not referred to in this study. Secondly, a discussion of the problem of application would stress the inescapable need for commentators to take a clear stand on these complicated issues. Thirdly, such a discussion would involve discussion of which interpretations are desirable. The answer depends on the answer to the important question of which purposes should be pursued. In my opinion, it should be both possible and desirable for scholars to fulfil Cranfield's critical purposes without at the same time making constructive interpretations and thus to avoid the tricky problem of application within the commentaries. The possibility of succeeding would increase if the differences between reconstructive and constructive interpretations and critical and creative purposes respectively were penetrated.

The importance of the problem of application in the commentaries by Barth, Nygren, Cranfield and Wilckens indicates that the question of how to relate reconstructive interpretations of scholarly exegesis to theological reflexion in a wider sense has yet to be satisfactorily answered. Furthermore, this is a problem not only of systematic theology or of the church. It is a problem which is integral to the biblical commentaries of Barth, Nygren, Cranfield and Wilckens and probably many other commentaries as well.

It seems to me that the problem of application is especially acute in the commentaries on such a central and theologically contentious text as that of

Romans. It also seems to me that there are several risks associated with the form of most biblical commentaries. Since the kinds of interpretations pursued, the combination of critical and creative purposes, the views of the content of faith and the fundamental questions concerning revelation, the view of the Bible and the problem of application are usually not developed explicitly, the interpretations of the biblical text become blurred. This study points to the need for a discussion of these issues in biblical commentaries which have both critical and creative purposes. Since commentaries which are exclusively critical are also likely to combine different kinds of interpretations and purposes, a good introduction to any commentary on Romans should deal not only with the date and place of writing etc, but also with the more basic questions of kinds of interpretations, purposes pursued and, when necessary, relevant basic theological issues. In this respect Barth's and Nygren's commentaries have advantages over those of Cranfield and Wilckens, since something of the sort is done in the introductions.

The complexity of the interpretations of Romans is fascinating in that we can conclude that different interpretations have been made possible by reference to different points of departure and different goals. Hopefully future insights and needs will provide us with new and better interpretations of the epistle Phoibe carried from Paul to the Romans. The task of mediating it beyond the city of Rome will continue to challenge her successors.

Summary

This thesis dealt with the problem of how it comes about that Paul's Epistle to the Romans receives different interpretations in the contemporary commentaries of Barth, Nygren, Cranfield and Wilckens. To find a solution to this problem it is necessary to answer two questions. First, how exactly do the commentaries differ from each other? and second, how can these differences be explained? The purpose of this study was (1) to set out and analyse the different interpretations of Romans given by Barth, Nygren, Cranfield and Wilckens and (2) to examine whether these differences can be explained and, if so, how.

The first purpose was dealt with in part one. The differences on which I focused concerned problems of interpretation with a relation to systematic theology, since it was argued that the different interpretations become important when they relate to central theological issues. The differences analysed concerned the three levels of the interpretation of Romans 7 (chapter one), interpretations of some theological themes (chapter two) and some general remarks on Romans (chapter three).

Analysis of Barth's, Nygren's, Cranfield's and Wilckens' interpretations of Romans 7 clearly showed that they put forward four different interpretations, each of which had distinctive features. Major differences were that Barth and Wilckens interpreted ἐγώ (I) as a person ante Christum, while Nygren and Cranfield held ἐγώ to be a Christian. Barth and Nygren also interpreted the law-concept in Romans 7 in a wider sense, while Cranfield and Wilckens took it to be the Torah. Cranfield and Wilckens furthermore held the law to be restored in life post Christum, while Barth and Nygren ascribed no prime function to the law in life post Christum.

The differences which were found in chapter two concerning some theological themes confirmed the conclusions of chapter one that Barth, Nygren, Cranfield and Wilckens give four different interpretations of Romans. Their interpretations point to four different doctrines of atonement. Some affinities were also clear between Barth's and Nygren's commentaries on the one hand and Cranfield's and Wilckens' on the other. According to Barth and Nygren, Romans contains a sharp dualism between this world and God's reality. Cranfield and Wilckens hold no such view and therefore interpret the relation between the old and the new covenants to be more harmonious than Barth and Nygren. Cranfield and Wilckens are, furthermore, more optimistic about the effect of righteousness in Christian life in this world than Barth and Nygren.

Concerning the general remarks on Romans, analysed in chapter three, the importance of knowledge of the historical situation of Paul and of the Romans is stressed in Cranfield's and Wilckens' commentaries, but not in Barth's and Nygren's. Cranfield and Wickens however differ in their descriptions of the situation. Furthermore, all four commentators agree that the theme of Romans was the way that human beings attain righteousness through faith in God's act in Christ. They nevertheless differ considerably about the key to the interpretation of this theme.

My second purpose, examining explanations for the different interpretations, was dealt with in part two. I took as my starting-point a theory of interpretation. Its main feature is that the process of interpretation is described in terms of the interpreter's choice between different possible interpretations by reference to different kinds of arguments: philological, contextual, historical, intentional, natural, consistency and constructive arguments. The different kinds of arguments are further understood as criteria of different kinds of interpretations. It was also argued that there is a fundamental difference between the first six kinds of interpretations and the last. The first kinds are called reconstructive interpretations in contrast to the constructive interpretations.

Explanations for the different interpretations given by Barth, Nygren, Cranfield and Wilckens are sought in the different kinds of interpretations (chapter four), the purposes of the commentaries (chapter five) and some basic assumptions made by the commentaries and revealed in the constructive arguments (chapter six).

The analysis in chapter four shows that all the commentators use several kinds of arguments, including both reconstructive and constructive arguments, for their interpretations. A pattern can be discerned in each commentary of an interpretive basis. The different interpretations can thus be explained in part by reference to the commentators' use of different kinds of arguments and to their content. Furthermore, it is argued that the historical and constructive arguments are decisive for the choice of interpretation while this is not true of the other kinds of arguments. The differences can thus be further explained in particular by the contents of the historical and constructive arguments. However, it is also shown that the commentaries lacked clear methodological strategies. Although not explaining the different interpretations per se, this observation strengthens the possibility of different interpretations.

In chapter five the different interpretations of the commentators are explained by their pursuit of different combinations of purposes. The purposes are said to be either critical or creative. The critical purposes are said to involve description and analysis of the text and to be hypothetical in character, while the creative purposes are held to concern the application of the text and to be closely related to faith and normative in character. Only Cranfield's purposes are exclusively critical, while Barth, Nygren and Wilckens combine critical and creative purposes in different ways. It is further stated that critical purposes are only compatible with reconstructive interpretations, while creative purposes require constructive interpretations. A comparison with the results of chapter four shows that only Barth fulfils his purposes, while Nygren, Cranfield and Wilckens fail in important respects. This result also helps explain how the different interpretations are possible, since it points to a basic lack of clarity in the commentaries.

In chapter six it is shown that the different interpretations by Barth, Nygren, Cranfield and Wilckens can also be explained by the differences between their understandings of the content of Christian faith. More basic assumptions however also play a part. These four commentaries point to four different non-propositional views of revelation. They also have different attitudes toward historical-critical scholarship. None has a secular attitude: all hold the Bible to be the word of God. This helps explain the frequency of the constructive arguments. Finally, it is shown that Barth, Nygren and Wilckens put forward different solutions to the problem of relating the reconstructive interpretations to the constructive, that is, the problem of application, and that these solutions all open the way for differences of interpretation.

Analysis of four examples of interpretations of the same text enabled me to scrutinize the process of interpretation. The knowledge of what the differences actually consist of and the observation that they are found on different levels provide a fruitful starting-point for theoretical reflection on biblical interpretation. Instead of putting forward general assumptions about the presuppositions underlying the commentaries analysed, I have been able to reveal a complicated network of different kinds of interpretations. Any simplified characterization of the commentaries as either dogmatic or historical has been shown to be impossible. I have also been able to qualify the general statement that the theology of the commentators guides their interpretations. By analysing the arguments given for their interpretations, I have been able to show in exactly what respects the theological assumptions of the commentators are influential. I have also been able to clarify the different characters of these assumptions, bearing either on the content of Christian faith or on more basic theological assumptions. Finally, I have been able to point to the problems connected with the relation between reconstructive and constructive interpretations, that is, the problem of application.

This dissertation points to the need to develop models to resolve the problem of application as a crucial problem of biblical interpretation. Such discussion would benefit from taking the same starting point in analysis of concrete examples of interpretations of biblical texts: e g exegetical monographs, other Bible commentaries, Old and New Testament theologies. Development of models in this way would imply discussion of different kinds of interpretations and possible methodological strategies for relating them to each other. It would also elucidate the different possibilities of combinations of purposes in biblical interpretation. Finally, development of application models would involve discussion of more basic issues concerning revelation and the view of the Bible. In all of these areas the empirical point of departure would necessitate the development of subtle distinctions which would help clarify the theoretical discussion of the problem of biblical interpretation.

Bibliography

Achtemeier, Paul J
1985   Romans, (Interpretation, A Bible Commentary for Teaching and Preaching), John Knox Press, Atlanta.

Althaus, Paul
1966   Der Brief an die Römer, (Das Neue Testament Deutsch. Neues Göttinger Bibelwerk, Teilband 6), 10th ed, Vandenhoeck and Ruprecht, Göttingen.

Baird, William
1981   "Recent Commentaries on Romans" in Religious Studies Review 7 (3/81), Waterloo, Ontario, pp 221–238.

Barr, James
1981a   Fundamentalism, 2nd ed, SCM Press Ltd, London.
1981b   "The Bible as a Document of Believing Communities" in Hans Dieter Betz (ed): The Bible as A Document of the University, (Polebridge Books no 3), Scholars Press, Chico, California, pp 25–47.
1983   The Bible in the Modern World, 4th ed, SCM Press, London.

Barrett, C K
1957   A Commentary on the Epistle to the Romans, (Black's New Testament Commentaries), Adam and Charles Black, London.

Barth, Karl
1919   Der Römerbrief, G A Bäschlin, Bern.
1926   Der Römerbrief, Vierter Abdruck der neuen Bearbeitung, 5th ed, Chr Kaiser Verlag, München.
1956   Kurze Erklärung des Römerbriefes, Chr Kaiser Verlag, München.

Betz, Hans Dieter (ed)
1981   The Bible as A Document of the University, (Polebridge Books no 3), Scholars Press, Chico, California.

Brown, Raymond E
1985   Biblical Exegesis and Church Doctrine, Paulist Press, New York, Mahwah, New Jersey.

Cranfield, Charles E B

1985　A Critical and Exegetical Commentary on the Epistle to the Romans, (The International Critical Commentary), Volume I, Introduction and Commentary on Romans I-VIII, 5th ed, T & T Clark Ltd, Edinburgh. (Cranfield 1985 (1))

1986　A Critical and Exegetical Commentary on the Epistle to the Romans, (The International Critical Commentary), Volume II, Commentary on Romans IX-XVI and Essays, 4th ed, T & T Clark Ltd, Edinburgh. (Cranfield 1986 (2))

1987　Romans, a Shorter Commentary, 3rd ed, T & T Clark Ltd, Edinburgh.

Dunn, James D G

1987　"The Task of New Testament Theology" in Dunn, James D G and Mackey, James P: New Testament Theology in Dialogue, (Biblical Foundations in Theology), SPCK, London, pp 1–26.

EKK Vorarbeiten

1969　Evangelisch-Katholischer Kommentar zum Neuen Testament. Vorarbeiten Heft 1, Neukirchener Verlag, Neukirchen and Benziger Verlag, Zürich, Einsiedeln, Köln.

1972　Evangelisch-Katholischer Kommentar zum Neuen Testament. Vorarbeiten Heft 4, Neukirchener Verlag, Neukirchen and Benziger Verlag, Zürich, Einsiedeln, Köln.

Epp, Eldon Jay and MacRae, George W (eds)

1989　The New Testament and Its Modern Interpreters, (The Bible and Its Modern Interpreters, ed Douglas A Knight), Fortress Press, Philadelphia, and Scholars Press, Atlanta.

Das Evangelium und die Kirche

1972　"Bericht der evangelisch-lutherisch/römisch-katholischen Studienkommission 'Das Evangelium und die Kirche' " in Lutherische Rundschau, Zeitschrift des Lutherischen Weltbundes, 22. Jahrgang, Heft 3, Kreuz Verlag, Stuttgart, pp 344–362.

Fornberg, Tord

1981　"Att tolka bibeltexter" in Grenholm, Carl-Henric (ed): Metoder för teologer. En handledning för religionsvetenskapligt studium, Studentlitteratur, Lund, pp 85–94.

Frye, Northrop

1982　The Great Code. The Bible and Literature, Routledge & Kegan Paul, London, Melbourne & Henley.

Fuller, Reginald H
1989 "New Testament Theology" in Epp, Eldon Jay and MacRae, George W (eds): The New Testament and Its Modern Interpreters, (The Bible and Its Modern Interpreters, ed Douglas A Knight), Fortress Press, Philadelphia, and Scholars Press, Atlanta, pp 565–584.

Furberg, Mats
1982 Säga, förstå, tolka. Till yttrandets och textens problem, Doxa, Lund.

Grant, Robert M with Tracy, David
1984 A Short History of the Interpretation of the Bible, Second Edition Revised and Enlarged, SCM Press, London.

Grenholm, Carl-Henric
1973 Christian Social Ethics in a Revolutionary Age. An Analysis of the Social Ethics of John C Bennett, Heinz-Dietrich Wendland and Richard Shaull, Acta Universitatis Upsaliensis, (Uppsala Studies in Social Ethics 1), Almqvist & Wiksell International, Stockholm.
1981 (ed) Metoder för teologer. En handledning för religionsvetenskapligt studium, Studentlitteratur, Lund.

Gunnlaugur, A Jónsson
1988 The Image of God. Genesis 1:26-28 in a Century of Old Testament Research, (Coniectanea Biblica, Old Testament Series 26), Almqvist & Wiksell International, Stockholm.

Harnack, Adolf v
1927 Das Wesen des Christentums. Sechzehn Vorlesungen vor Studierenden aller Fakultäten im Wintersemester 1899/1900 an der Universität Berlin, 4th ed, J C Hinrichs'sche Buchhandlung, Leipzig.

Hermerén, Göran
1982 "Tolkningstyper och tolkningskriterier" in Tolkning och tolkningsteorier. Föredrag och diskussionsinlägg vid Vitterhetsakademiens symposium 17-19 november 1981, (Konferenser 7), Kungl Vitterhets Historie och Antikvitets Akademien, Almqvist & Wiksell International, Stockholm, pp 269–292.

Hick, John
1973 Philosophy of Religion, (Foundations of Philosophy Series), 2nd ed, Prentice-Hall, Inc, Englewood Cliffs, New Jersey.

Holte, Ragnar
1984 Människa livstolkning gudstro. Teorier och metoder inom tros- och livsåskådningsvetenskapen, Doxa, Lund.

Ingebrand, Sven
1966   Bibeltolkningens problematik. En historisk översikt, 2nd ed, Diakoni-
        styrelsens bokförlag, Stockholm.

Jeffner, Anders
1981   Vägar till teologi, Skeab, Stockholm.
1982   "Dogmatik II. Dogmatik in den nordischen Ländern" in Wolter,
        Michael and Freitag-Otte, Gertrud (eds): Theologische Realenzyklo-
        pädie, Band IX, Walter de Gruyter, Berlin and New York, pp 77–92.

Kieffer, René
1984   "Vad innebär det att kommentera en text?" in Kieffer, René and
        Olsson, Birger (eds): Exegetik idag. Nya frågor till gamla texter,
        (Religio 11), 2nd ed, Teologiska institutionen, Lund, pp 113–120.

Kuss, Otto
1957   Der Römerbrief, 1. Teilband, (Regensburger Neues Testament), Ver-
        lag Friedrich Pustet, Regensburg.
1959   Der Römerbrief, 2. Teilband, (Regensburger Neues Testament), Ver-
        lag Friedrich Pustet, Regensburg.

Käsemann, Ernst
1973   An die Römer, (Handbuch zum Neuen Testament 8a), J C B Mohr
        (Paul Siebeck), Tübingen.

Leenhardt, Franz-J
1957   L'épitre de Saint Paul aux Romains, (Commentaire du Nouveau Testa-
        ment VI), Delachaux, Neuchatel, and Niestlé, S A, Paris.

Lindberg, Lars
1969   Omvändelsen i Karl Barths teologi, Gummessons, Stockholm.

Lohfink, Gerhard
1974   "Kommentar als Gattung. Rudolf Schnackenburg zum 60. Geburts-
        tag" in Bibel und Leben 15, Düsseldorf, pp 1–16.

Longman, Tremper III
1987   Literary Approaches to Biblical Interpretation, (Foundations of Con-
        temporary Interpretation Vol 3), Academie Books, Zonderwan
        Publishing House, Grand Rapids, Michigan.

Michel, Otto
1966   Der Brief an die Römer, (Kritisch-exegetischer Kommentar über das
        Neue Testament 4), 5th ed, Vandenhoeck and Ruprecht, Göttingen.

Morgan, Robert with Barton, John
1988   Biblical Interpretation, (Oxford Bible Series), Oxford University Press, Oxford.

Naess, Arne
1966   Communication and Argument. Elements of Applied Semantics, trans Alastair Hannay, Universitetsforlaget, Oslo, Allen & Unwin Ltd, London and The Bedminster Press, Totowa, New Jersey.

Noorda, Sijbolt Jan
1989   Historia Vitae Magistra. Een Beoordeling van de Geschiedenis van de uitleg van Lucas 4,16-30 als bijdrage aan de hermeneutische discussie, V U Uitgeverij, Amsterdam.

Nordlander, Agne
–   Rom 3:21-26 och försoningsläran. Unpublished manuscript.

Nygren, Anders
1930   Den kristna kärlekstanken genom tiderna. Eros och Agape. Första delen, Svenska kyrkans diakonistyrelses bokförlag, Stockholm.
1944   Pauli brev till romarna, (Tolkning av Nya Testamentet, band VI), Svenska kyrkans diakonistyrelses bokförlag, Stockholm.
1952   Commentary on Romans, trans Carl C Rasmussen, SCM Press Ltd, London.
1953   Agape and Eros. Part I: A Study of the Christian Idea of Love. Part II: The History of the Christian Idea of Love. Authorized translation by Philip S Watson, SPCK, London.

Olsson, Birger
1984   "Moderna bibelkommentarer och omoderna" in René Kieffer and Birger Olsson (eds): Exegetik idag. Nya frågor till gamla texter, (Religio 11), 2nd ed, Teologiska institutionen, Lund, pp 121–141.

Patte, Daniel
1983   Paul's Faith and the Power of the Gospel. A Structural Introduction to the Pauline Letters, Fortress Press, Philadelphia.

Perrin, Norman and Duling, Dennis C
1982   The New Testament, An Introduction, Proclamation and Parenesis, Myth and History, 2nd ed, Harcourt Brace Jovanovich Publishers, New York and London.

Pettersson, Torsten
1988   Literary Interpretation: Current Models and a New Departure, Åbo Academy Press, Åbo.

Reventlow, Henning Graf

1986   Problems of Biblical Theology in the Twentieth Century, SCM Press Ltd, London. (Trans of Hauptprobleme der Biblischen Theologie im 20. Jahrhundert.)

Richardson, Alan

1964   Creeds in the Making. A Short Introduction to the History of Christian Doctrine, 6th ed, SCM Press Ltd, London.

Ricoeur, Paul

1980   Essays on Biblical Interpretation. Edited with an Introduction by Lewis S Mudge, Fortress Press, Philadelphia.

Räisänen, Heikki

1987   Paul and the Law. (Wissenschaftliche Untersuchungen zum Neuen Testament 29), 2nd edition, revised and enlarged, J C B Mohr (Paul Siebeck), Tübingen.

Sanders, Ed P

1977   Paul and Palestinian Judaism. A Comparison of Patterns of Religion, Fortress Press, Philadelphia.

1983   Paul, the Law and the Jewish People, Fortress Press, Philadelphia.

Schenk, Wolfgang

1980   "Was ist ein Kommentar?" in Biblische Zeitschrift, Jahrgang 24, Heft 1, Paderborn, pp 1–20.

Schlier, Heinrich

1977   Der Römerbrief, (Herders theologischer Kommentar zum Neuen Testament, Band VI), Herder, Freiburg, Basel, Wien.

Shaw, Graham

1982   The Cost of Authority. Manipulation and Freedom in the New Testament, Fortress Press, Philadelphia.

Stendahl, Krister

1962   "Biblical theology, contemporary" in Buttrick, George Arthur (ed): The Interpreter's Dictionary of the Bible, An Illustrated Encyclopedia in Four Volumes, Vol I, Abingdon Press, New York and Nashville, pp 418–432.

1976   Paul Among Jews and Gentiles and Other Essays, Fortress Press, Philadelphia.

Stenström, Thure

1984   Existentialismen i Sverige. Mottagande och inflytande 1900-1950, Acta Universitatis Upsaliensis, (Historia litterarum 13), Almqvist & Wiksell International, Stockholm.

Stirewalt, Martin Luther Jr
1977 "The Form and Function of the Greek Letter-Essay" in Donfried, Karl P (ed): The Romans Debate, Essays by T W Manson, Günther Bornkamm, Karl P Donfried, Jacob Jervell, Robert J Karris, Wolfgang Wiefel, Martin Luther Stirewalt, Jr, Willhelm Wuellner and Günter Klein, Augsburg Publishing House, Minneapolis, pp 175–206.

Unger, Johan (ed)
1980 Såsom i en spegel. En debattbok om Paulusbilden och kristendomstolkningen. (Svenska kyrkans kulturinstituts Dialogserie 17), Skeab Dialog, Stockholm.

Wilckens, Ulrich
1978 Der Brief an die Römer, (Evangelisch-Katholischer Kommentar VI/1), 1. Teilband, Röm 1-5, Benziger Verlag, Zürich, Einsiedeln, Köln, and Neukirchener Verlag, Neukirchen-Vluyn. (Wilckens 1978 (1))
1980 Der Brief an die Römer, (Evangelisch-Katholischer Kommentar VI/2), 2. Teilband, Röm 6-11, Benziger Verlag, Zürich, Einsiedeln, Köln, and Neukirchener Verlag, Neukirchen-Vluyn. (Wilckens 1980 (2))
1982 Der Brief an die Römer, (Evangelisch-Katholischer Kommentar VI/3) 3. Teilband, Röm 12-16, Benziger Verlag, Zürich, Einsiedeln, Köln, and Neukirchener Verlag, Neukirchen-Vluyn. (Wilckens 1982 (3))

Wingren, Gustaf
1958 Theology in Conflict. Nygren – Barth – Bultmann, Trans Eric H Wahlstrom, Muhlenberg Press, Philadelphia.

Young, Frances
1989 "Exegetical Method and Scriptural Proof. The Bible in Doctrinal Debate" in Studia Patristica xix, Papers of the 1983 Oxford International Patristics Conference, Leuven, Belgium, pp 291–304.

Zeller, Dieter
1985 Der Brief an die Römer, (Regensburger Neues Testament), Verlag Friedrich Pustet, Regensburg.

Texts and translations

Quotations from the Bible are taken from:

Novum Testamentum Graece

1979   Eberhard Nestle & Kurt Aland (eds), 26th ed, Deutsche Bibelstiftung, Stuttgart.

The Holy Bible

1962   The Oxford Annotated Bible, Revised Standard Version, Herbert G May and Bruce M Metzger (eds), Oxford University Press, Oxford.

Index of persons